Hard Zen, Soft Heart

Other Titles from Falcon Press

Christopher S. Hyatt, Ph.D.
Undoing Yourself With Energized Meditation & Other Devices
Radical Undoing: Complete Course for Undoing Yourself (DVDs)
Energized Hypnosis (book, CDs & DVDs)
To Lie Is Human: Not Getting Caught Is Divine
The Psychopath's Bible: For the Extreme Individual
Secrets of Western Tantra: The Sexuality of the Middle Path

Christopher S. Hyatt, Ph.D. with contributions by
Wm. S. Burroughs, Timothy Leary, Robert A. Wilson, et al.
Rebels & Devils: The Psychology of Liberation

S. Jason Black and Christopher S. Hyatt, Ph.D.
Pacts With the Devil: A Chronicle of Sex, Blasphemy & Liberation
Urban Voodoo: A Beginner's Guide to Afro-Caribbean Magic

Lon Milo DuQuette & Christopher S. Hyatt, Ph.D.
Aleister Crowley's Illustrated Goetia

Christopher S. Hyatt, Ph.D. & Antero Alli
A Modern Shaman's Guide to a Pregnant Universe

Antero Alli
Angel Tech: A Modern Shaman's Guide to Reality Selection

Israel Regardie
The Complete Golden Dawn System of Magic
The Golden Dawn Audios

Joseph C. Lisiewski, Ph.D.
Israel Regardie and the Philosopher's Stone
Ceremonial Magic and the Power of Evocation
Kabbalistic Cycles and the Mastery of Life
Howlings from the Pit

Sorceress Cagliastro
Blood Sorcery Bible Volume 1: Rituals in Necromancy

Peter J. Carroll
The Chaos Magick Audio CDs
PsyberMagick

Phil Hine
Condensed Chaos
Prime Chaos
The Pseudonomicon

**For up-to-the-minute information on prices and
availability, please visit our website at
http://originalfalcon.com**

Hard Zen, Soft Heart

by
Christopher S. Hyatt, Ph.D.
&
Diana Rose Hartmann, M.A.

THE *Original* FALCON PRESS
TEMPE, ARIZONA, U.S.A.

International Standard Book Number: 978-1-935150-97-8 (Print Edition)
ISBN: 978-1-61869- 970-1 (mobi)
ISBN: 978-1-61869-971-8 (ePub)

Library of Congress Catalog Card Number: 98-84916

First Edition (Print and eBook) 2013

The paper used in this publication meets the minimum requirements of
the American National Standard for Permanence of Paper for Printed
Library Materials Z39.48-1984

Address all inquiries to:
THE ORIGINAL FALCON PRESS
1753 East Broadway Road #101-277
Tempe, AZ 85282 U.S.A.
(or)
PO Box 3540
Silver Springs, NV 89429 U.S.A.

website: http://www.originalfalcon.com
email: info@originalfalcon.com

In the beginner's mind there are many possibilities. In the expert's mind there are few.

— Suzuki Roshi

If there is a remedy when trouble strikes,
What reason is there for despondency?
And if there is no help for it,
What is the use of being sad?

So come what may, I'll never harm
My cheery happiness of mind.
Depression never brings me what I want...
My virtue will be warped and marred by it.

— Nagarjuna

The authentic self is the best part of a human being. It's the part of you that already cares, that is already passionate about evolution. When your authentic self miraculously awakens and becomes stronger than your ego, then you will truly begin to make a difference in this world. You will literally enter into a partnership with the creative principle.

— Andrew Cohen

We live in a house of mirrors and think we are looking out the windows.

— Fritz Perls

TABLE OF CONTENTS

PART I
WHERE AM I GOING AND HOW WILL I KNOW I'VE ARRIVED WHEN I MAKE IT THERE?

PART II
THE PRACTICE OF PUTTING YOURSELF ON

PART III
THE ENDLESS MEDITATION

INTRODUCTION

by Nicholas Tharcher

If you are a fan of Christopher Hyatt's work, you are probably aware that the publication of *Hard Zen, Soft Heart* has been a long time coming. Though it is just now being released in 2013—five years after Hyatt's death—the first drafts were written in the 1990s. It has gone through several revisions, three editors and a recent revisitation by co-author Diana Rose Hartmann.

The focus of the book has changed several times over its history. At one time the authors envisioned it as a "Zen" book in the "hit you over the head" style of Hyatt's classic *Undoing Yourself with Energized Meditation and Other Devices*. But because some readers have criticized Hyatt's work as too "hard hitting" and "demanding" the authors came to envision *Hard Zen* in an entirely different way: as a more "gentle" entrée into Dr. Hyatt's work, something that a wider audience could connect with. However, before the book was finished circumstances changed.

Hyatt had always been dissatisfied with the inability of the written word to convey the details of the many physical exercises that were key to his methods. When, around the time that *Hard Zen* was being written, new audio and video technology became more accessible, Hyatt finally felt able to demonstrate his methods through these media, and he switched his attention to the development of the *Radical Undoing* and *Energized Hypnosis* series. So *Hard Zen* sat on the shelf...until now.

For those who are not familiar with Hyatt's work, it will become clear very quickly that—"gentle" as the approach of this book may be—Hyatt was fundamentally an elitist who recognized that most people are satisfied to live "a life of quiet desperation" rather than undertake the difficult process of transcending the consequences of the ragtag physiology that evolution has built.

As a trained scientist, Hyatt gave great credence to the remarkable work done over the past few years on the structure and physiology of the human brain in order to better understand the true nature of homo sapiens and the future of the human species. He concluded that, in its current form, it has no future. Only by conscious, deliberate re-engineering—essentially creating an entirely new species with a very different brain structure—can homo normalis be anything but a dead end. The technology to do this is almost here and, among a few, there is the will to do it. Whether this can be done in a world so terrified of itself, only time will tell. (Science fiction writers have investigated this theme many times...and in their stories the outcome does not generally go well...)

However, for the species as it is today there are a few techniques that can help rewire (some) brains to (some) degree and improve the overall condition of (some) mutant individuals (somewhat)...but those methods require a great deal of time, dedication and focus—something most are not prepared to do.

If you are among those few that Hyatt considered the true elite, you are probably "successful" already and may not need his methods...unless you want to become even more than you are now. However, if you are among the 10% or so of the human population that is "in between"—capable of more but living a dead-end life—Hyatt's work can have immense value for you...if you are willing to work at it.

Hyatt's methods are neither a rehash of some obscure mystical practices nor a bunch of New Age feel-good platitudes. As both an expert occultist and trained scientist Hyatt had no use for such nonsense...and neither should you. Hyatt cared only about one thing: Does it work?

His methods were originally developed in the 1970s in collaboration with his longtime friend and mentor Dr. Israel Regardie. Though Regardie may be best known as a one-time confidant of Aleister Crowley and for his work in the mystical system called the Golden Dawn, he was also a practicing psychotherapist who made extensive use of (neo-)Reichian techniques. Together Hyatt and Regardie created a system which is now available to the layman through Hyatt's many books, audios and videos.

The system incorporates breathing and meditation techniques that have been used for millennia as well as many of the body-centered and hypnotic techniques that were developed during the 20th century. Together, these techniques *work!*

Following the original intent of the book, *Hard Zen* opens with a chapter taken from the earliest editions of *Undoing Yourself*: "To Know Enlightenment, Not Just To Know Of It". And fittingly, the book closes with another chapter from *Undoing Yourself*, Diana Hartmann's "Eris: Chaos as Prerequisite to Change". Between those chapters you will find numerous insights into the workings of your brain and valuable methods to improve its functioning. If you choose to jump into the deep end of Hyatt's system, you will find even more: the means to transcend.

FOREWORD

To live life authentically you must first gain awareness of what causes you to react in ways that sabotage your happiness. When you learn to respond to life without being weighed down by the chains of your subconscious and your past, you will experience true freedom. Freedom from self-defeating habits, painful relationships, chronic anxiety, and even despair. With a bit of self-awareness, you will learn to crack the shell of your false self.

A new creature—your authentic Self—waits to be born again! A sense of wonder will prevail. Like a child, you will begin to perceive the world without the shades of past traumas or future worries. Free to be your Self and live in the moment, life becomes a magical, mystical adventure of bliss and love.

Bill Shakespeare, who wrote many plays about unhappy people who had lost their true Selves, typically sent his discontented characters into a magical forest where, temporarily free from the trappings and deceit of civilization, they would shed their false selves (ego) and learn to live authentically. (A famous exception is, of course, Hamlet, who said: "This above all: To thine own self be true.") The quest to find one's authentic Self is timeless.

In "As You Like It", a young Duke awakens to his authentic Self in the Forest of Arden and exclaims (paraphrased):

> Are not these woods more free from peril than the envious
> court? Here feel we but...the seasons' difference...the icy
> fang...of the winter's wind,
> which bites and blows upon my body,
> 'till I shrink with cold... (Even so) I smile and say
> "This is no flattery: these are (advisors)
> that feelingly (teach) me what I am."
> ...And this our life exempt from public haunt,
> Finds tongues in trees, books in the running brooks,
> Sermons in stones, and good in every thing.

Take the journey! What do you have to lose but your falseness, misery and pain?

When you crawl out of the shell your subconscious built to protect yourself from harm during times of trauma, you begin to live with conscious awareness. Each moment becomes wondrously new. This is the Bliss of Life.

Existential ennui—the great horror of inauthentic life—and the painful cycle of tension-crisis-relief-tension, ends. As you learn to be true to your authentic self, you attain the courage to fulfill your potential, acquire inner peace, and keep your calm center, even when life throws punches.

Sadly, most of us spend our entire lives imprisoned by the past or obsessing about the future. Fear of the future is the primary cause of greed and hoarding, which causes more speculation and an increasing compulsiveness to do anything to numb ourselves from chronic tension. Miserable and terrorized by our fantasies of the future, we spend what we would save for a relaxing vacation on insurance and bonds...just in case.

You might ask yourself, "Why are we all so screwed up?" The answer is simple. Most of us are puppets of automatic reactions that were created due to our past experiences or traumas. Even when we consciously work to be happier, we often end up in the same muddle. It isn't our fault, but there it is all the same.

The pattern is frustrating to say the least.

If you want to truly LIVE, then you must don the hat of a Brain Change Technician. You DO have the power to change your life. You just need to enter the Forest of Your Subconscious, find and pull out the roots of a few overgrown trees or weeds, and cultivate your Self by feeding your Self with words of confidence, love and self-forgiveness. Drink of the water of Life and learn to be fluid. Use your pruning shears and Stay Alert, nipping the Weeds of Doubt in the bud.

There is no need to be chained to lifelong therapy, pain, drugs or methods that offer temporary relief for a month's paycheck. With self-awareness and work, you can become the content and amazing human you want to be.

However, most of us spend our lives imprisoned by past memories. In a sense, we are the sum of our experiences and memories, for better or worse. But, no matter how painful or traumatic your past was, you need not continue to suffer or repeat self-defeating behaviors. With a little work, you can become freer and happier.

Most humans are unconscious puppets of automatic reactions caused by past experiences or traumas. Changing that may seem difficult. How many times have you strived for a happier future, only to end up in the same stressful state? The circumstances and players have changed, you tried your best, and yet here you are again, feeling worse than ever because now you blame yourself for each failure.

Take heart and rid yourself of guilt and shame. It wasn't *You* who failed. Conscious attempts to change using sheer willpower are rarely successful due to the subterfuge and sabotage of your subconscious programming. In other words, it is your past memories, hidden deep in the basement of your mind, which prevent you from reaching your full potential.

As noted in the film *Induction*, your subconscious is **powerful** and gets angry when you (i.e., your conscious mind) attempts to either change or introduce a new idea. A classical metaphor is Jacob Marley in Dickens' *A Christmas Carol*...whose ghost wears literal chains of his past...

The purpose of this book is threefold. Firstly, to provide you with information that will help you become aware of the subconscious programming that has prevented you from attaining your goals and finding peace of mind. Secondly, to offer you tools so you can change those behaviors and reactions which, due to your subconscious programming, cause you to constantly re-enact the past. And, thirdly, to help you manage your cerebral pharmacy and become a first class Brain Change Artist.

Once you are free from the chains of the past, you become free to change. The exercises herein will teach you to be AWARE of your chains, and learn to Be Here Now. Like all desirable things, breaking lifelong patterns takes effort and work. But if you truly want to be free, if you wish to live authentically and feel comfortable in your own skin, give your Self the beautiful gift of your Self! Diligently practice the exercises in this book. There is no time like the present, so let's get started.

To Know Enlightenment, Not Just To Know Of It

A Zen Statement

You must give up the thing most precious to you.
　　You must give up the thing which you love so dearly,
the thing that you hold on to
– You must give it up –
– You must give it up. –

There are no tricks to find
　　ENLIGHTENMENT.
It is not hiding anywhere.
It is HERE and NOW.

You must see that you are frightened,
that something is at STAKE all the time.
Even in your dreams—something is at stake.
ALL THE TIME.

Anything that shocks or disrupts or disturbs You is a helpful
　　friend.
Everything which allows you to sleep,
to be complacent,
will hinder You.

To become in Accordance with your
　　TRUE POTENTIAL,
you must be in Discordance with your self.

YOUR SELF IS LITERALLY AT STAKE—READY TO BE
　　BURNED—ALL THE TIME
　　　　YET, YOU COMPULSIVELY LOOK FOR FOOD WHICH
　　　　　　FEEDS YOU

Anything which delays your END
    feeds you.
You digest this diet overabundant with
    FAT.
You are insatiable and require constant
    FAT to keep you going.
You use more energy and power
    maintaining THE ILLUSION
of your insatiable dream than Living.
You will even STRUT to death's
window.

But to Know the DEATHLESS
    ONE —
you—**the strutter—must die.**
You must go on a diet—then
starve your false self to DEATH.

You must pull yourself in misery
in cranial pride and historic
    stupidity.

You must stop strutting around
    like a fattened COW.

You must stop bowing down to
    your mistakes.
You must stop your idol
    worshipping.
You must surrender your misery.

You must stop acting surprised when
  something "bad" happens to you

FOR — it is the same old thing.
  You must stop reacting to things
  By habit.
You must stop proving your story.
  You must stop extending the past
  into the present or your future
              will never change.

You must stop defending your stupidity,
— YOUR SLEEP.
You must stop defending
YOUR MISERY.

YOU MUST WAKE UP

You forsake Your Body Mind and Soul to feed this Monster.
He drinks Your blood,
this friend of yours.
you will sacrifice anything and everything to feed him.

Everyone and everything is food for you.
Whether people treat you good or bad is food for you.
you are so weak yet He is so strong.
Why do you prefer the insatiable one to HIM?

you oppose — you conform — all is food for you
you agree — you disagree — all is food for you.
you render opinions on everything
you spout authorities to back up your arguments,
Proving what cannot be Proved to keep your Mind Occupied.
Not knowing that the Country of your Body Mind Soul will soon
    be completely Occupied by the Fascists you invited in.
And Still...

— All is food for you.
You are surrounded by friends or alone —
— All is food for you.
You are naked or adorned —
— All is food for you.

SOMETHING IS **ALWAYS**
AT STAKE
SOMETHING IS ALWAYS
    ON THE LINE.

You strut around
proudly depressed of the misery
you have caused yourself.
You will do anything to preserve
    the misery.
You will fight,
you will sneer,
you will accuse,
you will blame,
you will steal, you will hide,
—all to preserve fear!
REMEMBER
THERE IS ALWAYS
SOMETHING
AT STAKE.
THAT SOMETHING IS YOU

nothing can satiate
wealth can not
fame can not
love can not
power can not
friends can not

ONLY ∞

AFTER YOU HAVE IT ALL, THEN WHAT?

victories feed you
your failures feed you
your past feeds you
your ideas feed you

if your friends allow you to be
    complacent,
accept or like you that is food
    for you.
If they hate you, that is food for
    you.

WHY ARE YOU SO HUNGRY?

Does death not even inspire your appetite?
Do you know death?
Or do you just have snapshots of it?
You act like you are immune from it,
that it just happens all around you
— but not to you.
Not even your own death can shudder you
move you from your — feeding frenzy.
As long as you can EAT, your death seems far, far away.

WHAT FOOD IS NEXT?

Misery is food,
and you can find plenty of that.
You are never at a loss for that.

You never learn
because MISERY is food.
You repeat the same mistake,
the same mistake, the same misery
over and over.

Worst of all
you repeat your misery with *pride*,
with your sneer of superiority,
WITH A SENSE OF NEWNESS,
with a sense of uniqueness,
with a sense of choice,
or with a sense of helplessness.

Yet, it is the same mistake,
the same misery.

You do not even dare find a NEW MISTAKE,
    A NEW MISERY

since that might wake you up from your
    FEEDING FRENZY

EXERCISE

In the beginning was the Word...

Words, whether thought or spoken, are immensely powerful. The first step to awareness is to notice the words you use. When you speak to others, pay attention to your language, particularly automatic phrases. (For example, when a colleague asks you how you are, note that you automatically reply "fine" or "life sucks" or whatever your automatic reply is.) As you begin to watch your language, you might notice that much of what you say is habit. You're still speaking and thinking in the same manner as you were years ago! Repetitive or automatic speaking are indications that you are sound asleep, even if you believe that you are having a conversation. Each time you repeat these habitual phrases, you reaffirm the *self* that you're comfortable with, the *self* that feels safe, even if this *self* is miserable. **This is the *self* that is chained by the past.**

DO THIS NOW!

Write down the patterns and phrases which you use most often. Then begin to become aware of HOW MANY TIMES you use these same phrases as if you were a programmed voice on a customer service phone system. (We assume that you have experienced the frustration of communicating with automatic telephone responses.) Have you ever wondered why you use these dead phrases over and over again? Why are they so dear to you?

Once you have made a list of the phrases, count the number of times you use them in a three-day period—you'll probably be amazed—and then:

STOP

STOP

STOP

STOP

Stay Awake
and each time you prepare to repeat
this DEAD WORD, this DEATH KNELL - - -

STOP

Say Stop to yourself.
Each time this stammered crippled phrase
rears Its Frightened head

STOP

BE SILENT.

Then, if you truly desire to know who and what you are,

REPLACE those DEAD PHRASES with Silence

Or... (while you practice)

SILENTLY TELL YOURSELF TO:

WAKE — UP !

BURSTING THE BUBBLE OF PERCEPTION

And even now the time seems remote when artistic energies and the practical wisdom of life will join with scientific thinking to form a higher organic system in relation to which scholars, physicians, artists and legislators—as we know them at present—would have to look like paltry relics of ancient times.
— Friedrich Nietzsche, *The Gay Science*, 1887

The peculiar human need to give meaning to life—to justify existence—to find God—to understand immediately—melts away at the moment of grand insight.
— C.S. Hyatt, Ph.D. 1993

PART I

WHERE AM I GOING AND HOW WILL I KNOW I'VE ARRIVED WHEN I MAKE IT THERE?

"It's the End of the World As You Know It"

The evolutionary progression of the last 3000 years has been aimed toward the development of the autonomous individual.

We humans worked hard to separate ourselves from the very Nature from which we were begotten. In fact, over the years, we have become so accustomed to being separated from Nature that we have *forgotten* our authentic Selves.

However, many physicists, such as Brianne Swimm and Fred Alan Wolf, are proposing that humans are now claiming a "cosmic" connection—a connection that is based on the sensing of a point (usually felt in the heart) that connects us all.

Cosmic kinship does not mean that we are regressing into archaic consciousness, but rather that we are progressing onto a wholly new path: a true relationship with Nature, both outward and inward.

A new door of perception has been opened.

Humans are entering into a new state of being, one which allows us to become artists of the world and, simultaneously, the artists of our Selves.

This is unlike our prior relationship with Nature, in which we lived according to what Nature bestowed upon us. Then we rose to a state of dominion over Nature—separating ourselves from Nature with the goal to conquer it. A cosmic-oriented human acts as a *Co-Creator* of the world. We merge with that which created nature and become attuned to creation itself. We begin to bestow on Nature (including our fellow humans) what we were previously only able to receive!

This is an amazing evolution! Where once we were prone to conform Nature to our (mostly false) definitions of ourselves, now Nature—or, our given environment—becomes a reflection of ourselves while we simultaneously reflect our environment.

Our environment has ceased to be Other. It has become, to borrow a technological term, *interactive*—with neither humans nor Nature having a position of superiority.

This means that we must become responsible to Nature. For if 90% of humans cling to the idea of being superior to Nature and continue to perceive Nature as Other, the road to enlightenment will become long and fraught with suffering. This long road might feel "normal" because it seems familiar. *And some will cling to misery because it's familiar and, therefore, safe.*

Wouldn't you rather **correct** yourself quickly and live joyfully in the present than wait until evolution kicks you into the gutter? Or until you're dead? Or reincarnated into an even more hellish world?

One way or another, this CHANGE WILL OCCUR!

It is your choice to speed up your evolution and live in peace and joy sooner, or cling to your old habits and suffer until someone else does the work.

Keep in mind that evolving into a New Person *does not* mean that we must forfeit our individuality. It does not mean you must think or do as others who are evolving. Quite the contrary, it means evolving into your unique potential!

Indeed, as many a cyberpunk prophet has attested, we may be moving towards a world wherein an independent external *reality* becomes a myth and virtual reality is the field upon which we play. And playing is fun!

It is also interesting to note that post-structural philosophers such as Foucault, Derrida and Deleuze posit a similar view of the world and Self.

The metaphysical structure upon which the Western World is founded is dissolving. Aristotelian-Platonic ideas—which presuppose a perfect and constant reality hiding behind the curtain of the temporal world—don't hold up to the scrutinizing eye of either modern philosophy or physics. Consequently, we are left with a *reality* which is mutable and deliciously mysterious.

Living in a world where change is the only constant seems frightening and often evokes feelings of insecurity, yet it also presents us with unlimited opportunity. A lack of constancy allows an infinite field of raw substance which we can mold—if we so choose.

And while science now is proving that change is the only constant, thousands of years ago, in the *Parinirvana* Sutra, Buddha wrote:

> *O bhikshus! Do not grieve! Even if I were to live in the world for as long as a kalpa, our coming together would have to end.*

*You should know that all things in the world are impermanent;
coming together inevitably means parting. Do not be troubled, for this
is the nature of life.*

*Diligently practicing right effort, you must seek liberation immedi-
ately. Within the light of wisdom, destroy the darkness of ignorance.
Nothing is secure. Everything in this life is precarious.*

*Always wholeheartedly seek the way of liberation. All things in the
world, whether moving or non-moving, are characterized by disappear-
ance and instability.*

*Stop now! Do not speak! Time is passing. I am about to cross over.
This is my final teaching.*

Robert Anton Wilson noted that there are more enlightened people living today than there were in Buddha's time. He calls this evolution the "Jumping Jesus Phenomenon" (although it has little to do with Christianity). Wilson stated that as each decade passes, the number of enlightened humans increases exponentially. But as a holy man once said, "The closer one becomes to God, the more demons will try to pull you down."

Even so, those who put in the work become alike to gods, if you will. The creative and brave can learn to walk on water, and become akin to the shamans, prophets, sages, gurus and other meta-humans who in the past have tried, time and time again, to teach us.

The most important thing is proper Intent. Once the intent is there, the evolutionary forces of Nature—both within us and without—will be set in motion.

Those who have researched the occultists might note that many novel "discoveries" of modern science are old hat. Magicians, alchemists and heretical groups that flourished during the Renaissance and the Age of Enlightenment taught and lived such wisdom ages ago; they just didn't have the technology to prove it. (And, if they did, they often kept their mouths shut for fear of being burned at the stake.)

But as a teacher of mine declared, "In those days, it wasn't time for the hidden wisdom to be revealed."

Now the time has come.

If humans do not wake up, we will become more isolated, frightened, depressed and sorrowful until we are forced by Nature herself to awaken!

It is your choice whether to speed up the process and mitigate the pain, or continue to live like an ostrich with its head in the sand.

<hr>

Of course, accepting the role as Architect or Artist of your world and your Self is a heavy responsibility.

While we all live in our own separate realities, these individual realities are part of a greater whole. If we are to survive as a species, we need to act in ways which will ensure the survival of our environment.

So we must go our merry individual ways *together*, as we journey toward a new world, one wherein our perceptions are cleansed and we perceive Nature and Ourselves as *interdependent* rather than separate. We must harbor the intent to cast off old, useless habits of the past, become heroes, and clear the way for the path of our heart, the path of our true Nature, the path to becoming alike to the Force that is LIFE!

TASK #1: BECOME A HERO

Most people are not free.
Freedom frightens them.
They follow patterns set by their parents, enforced by society
and by a constant inner dialog that weighs duty against desire
and pronounces duty the winner.
— Erica Jong, *Playboy*, March 1993

A hero, Jong goes on to say, is someone who has conquered his or
her fears.

When setting out to become a hero, all of us need to remember
that most heroes were not raised to be fearless. If they were, it was
through humiliation and founded on family pride, rather than
actual courage. (The word "courage" is derived from the French
"couer" and literally means "big heart.") Potential heroes must
unlearn habitual patterns—most of the time by painful
experiences or dark nights of the soul—if they are to finally overcome their fears.

The cowardly lion in *The Wizard of Oz* did not receive his courage from the Wizard. His courage was earned during his *journey*
to the wizard and the risks he took to aid his companions. It was
his love for his companions that gave him the courage to risk his
own life.

A frequently overlooked fear is the fear of freedom.

But one cannot become a hero until the fear of freedom is overcome, for a hero is not so much about becoming an extraordinary
man or woman, but as simply knowing your Self.

Sadly, most of us are so involved with identities which were
chosen for us by the various constituents of our upbringing that
we think we're doing what we want when, in reality, we've never
bothered to find out what we really want, or for that matter, who
we really are. Or, we're aware that we are doing what was chosen
for us, but are too afraid or too old or too defeated to attempt the
journey at all.

The most important thing you can do for your life, and the lives of your fellow beings, is to summon the will to endure the journey toward Self, whether that Self is ever found or not.

In fact, there is really no ONE Self to know.

Rather, we express a fluid succession of selves, ever-changing in accordance with our environment, the people we hang out with, and the tasks at hand.

Are we to assume then that we are a race of schizophrenics?

Hardly. And to avoid confusion, for the purposes of this book, we'll still use the singular when referring to your "Self". Just remember that Self is NOT static, but changing.

The Authentic Self—liquid, mutable and indefinable—is the key to freedom. However, this open state of existence elicits fear, in both our selves and our associates. We tend to relate sanity with *permanence*—those who change their points of view throughout their lives typically don't win elections.

Another example which makes this particular theory of the fluid or changing Self worth pondering is how our Self—meaning the particular way we perceive our world—changes dramatically during the course of LOVE!

When you are in the first stages of love, you are literally high. Flowers seem brighter. Workloads lighten. If you pay attention, you might even note that goals are accomplished. The boss gives you a promotion. You sense that you are aligned to Nature. Seemingly "magickal" coincidences occur. You feel blissful and you attract things you desire with little effort.

Anyone who has been dumped or betrayed by a lover will attest to the sense of loss of self. What was beautiful yesterday is now dull. The illusion of loss of self can be so dramatic that sometimes the heartbroken party becomes catatonic, or even commits suicide.

Perhaps the lovelorn could lessen the time spent in mourning if s/he realized that s/he is not mourning the loss of a partner, but rather *an aspect* of the self which was, in fact, created by the relationship. This aspect of self vanishes with the termination of the relationship, and as such, grieving is a natural emotional response.

Have you ever wondered what your life would be if you could WILL your self to be in a state of LOVE without being *dependent* on a significant other? To be in a state of love with your own Self, as well as the Self of everyone and everything? To find that point in your heart and know that you are connected to the point in the hearts of all humankind? Crowley wrote, "Love is the Law; Love under Will." In other words, the ability to will your Self into a state of love.

Love, of course, means being interconnected. To evolve into a state of interconnectedness where you might give without expecting a return, is a type of Love that heals, and brings joy!

Consider how many times you've been miserably disappointed when you did not get a pay-off for bestowing gifts of love or charity? But if you were expecting something in return, was your gift freely given?

The answer is no, for a gift that is given from Love—whether of emotion, time, or corporeal—is given without requiring a return.

There are no guarantees.

This type of love is both whole and holy, and is not dependent on the Other to bring joy. And if we can "Will" ourselves to this state of love in everything we do, we will find ourselves in a literal heaven on earth, in a state of constant meditation, love and ecstasy.

Mystics describe this as the ecstatic state that comes from giving their hearts and self to God (in any of His various faces). Yet even great mystics are beset by the demons of doubt. And when that happens, the "dark night of the soul" commences. And there one will stay until the Self can purify itself of its attachments to suffering and *will* itself to love once again.

And a great lover, a lover purified of the perceptions of the "false" self, will become a hero, a chivalric champion of human evolution and the Authentic Self!

—————•◇•—————

The hero of the Authentic Self also remains liquid enough to adapt to a world which seems to be changing at an exponential rate, but continues to self-govern himself. This means that we must utilize the Will to govern the Self.

So how does one become fluid and utilize one's Will simultaneously?

Consider a favorite metaphor of Taoism: the river. The river is its own master, yet it is intelligent enough to both move around the mountain and transform the shape of the mountain.

The river simultaneously forms and conforms. It knows the secret of the Both/And universe hailed by quantum mechanics and brain-change magicians.

THE HUNGRY GHOSTS OF PAST AND FUTURE

Don Juan tells Carlos Castaneda that we live in a "bubble of perception." We know our world through past experiences which reach out to meet our ever-changing and expanding universe. Or, as Alvin Reines put it: "The sense of reality is first of all constituted of experiences from a person's entire being: the senses, reason, desires and emotions; both the conscious and unconscious."

Karl Pribram, the neuro-psychologist, demonstrated that in addition to the neurological feedback system comprised by our past experiences, we also possess a *feed-forward* system.

This means that previous beliefs, memories and emotions *move forward* to modify incoming information *before* we are even conscious of it. This means that our past affects our present and our future, for better or worse.

Dr. Pribram suggests that our brain automatically unites new information (reality free from our personal "filters") with past information (subconscious memories). Our past experience defines how we perceive our present reality. Depending on our prior experiences, as our memories collide with the yet unprocessed information of our immediate futures, the result can sometimes be quite painful. Worse, since we are unaware of why a seemingly innocuous experience causes us to suffer, we don't know how to heal ourselves.

What we have believed or experienced throughout our lives *actively* interferes and restructures *WHAT* we see, experience and believe *NOW*.

We live in a world of hopeful expectation. On the one hand, we hope for a better life; on the other, we are aware that it is frightening to change, even if that change is for the good.

The core of meditative and self-awareness practice is to liberate ourselves from the filters and blinders that prevent us from perceiving our infinite interdependence and connectedness. However, most people would rather hold on to the beliefs that they were taught—no matter how painful and limiting—rather than step into the unknown.

Clinging to belief systems or outdated models of reality allows us to sleep soundly at night, even though we hope—and sometimes pray—for something to happen that will give us some control over the painful events of the past that continually effect our lives. We desperately want to know the future, yet at the same time are horrified by the prospects of the ensuing boredom. In other words, too much change can be devastating, while too little change leads to ennui and apathy. If the future is already written, why bother?

This being the case, most of us would rather jump from crisis to crisis, no matter how much we suffer, rather than fall into a state of boredom and apathy.

As you read this, you might be agreeing or noticing how, even in your own life, you prefer pain to either crucial change or apathy. But do you wonder why most people choose to live their entire lives locked in misery?

The reason is fairly obvious if you read newspapers. Most humans are motivated by fear and greed, usually simultaneously. Even those who claim to be motivated by honor or the need for respect often do so because they are greedy for honor or accolades from society, or because they fear losing status if they do not do "good". Some people might only fear the wrath of their vision of God, while simultaneously desiring that God love them "better" than others.

WHEN YOU'RE IN PAIN, OPIATES CAN BE A GOOD THING

Religion has helped humankind deal with death, pain and aging by providing security and assuring people that if they "act in a certain way" they will enjoy a reward in an *Afterlife*. We can see that religion has been a necessary opiate as it gave—and still gives—the suffering masses a reason to endure their earthly hells. Yet, while religion provides us with security and hope *after* life, we continually search for ways to realize our hopes and desires in our present lives.

In the past couple of centuries, science has juxtaposed itself against all religious beliefs, doubting everything, including itself. Science is the belief system of a man who says that faith, God and unassisted nature are not enough to give him comfort. The true scientist is a trickster: an authentic, playful, present human.

Modern science rebels against all absolute models. It says NO to groundless assertions. But this "no" is not a rejection of the numinous. (Numinous refers to a state in which one perceives something that cannot be known by the five ordinary senses.) In fact, noted scientists, such as Carl Sagan, have discussed the importance of separating the numinous from the supernatural.

Nevertheless, what is now a modern science of uncertainty emerged from man as an objective tool to destroy assertions and dogma fueled by belief. Revealing our Authentic Self also requires that we challenge our beliefs and perception, but unlike science, it focuses on subjective experience.

The amount of energy and money put into medical research alone are enough to prove man's dislike for anything which seems inevitable, particularly disease, death and pain. Even so, it's likely that when faced with great pain or death, humans will hope to be healed by medical science while praying for a supernatural "miracle."

This ongoing pattern is based on the motivators of greed and fear. Greed for a God-like power over life and death. Fear of letting go of the security of the afterlife.

A hundred years ago cloning, genetic science, organ transplants and wonder drugs would have been regarded as heresy by some and madness by others.

Why?

Simply stated, what is considered heresy or madness is merely that which is outside of our current definitions of reality.

Old habits die hard.

Another example is matter. In ancient times, some believed matter to be an inactive substance, while others believed it to be active and, therefore, living. Now we know that matter is very active. However, we do not consider matter to be alive...as we currently understand the word "alive." Or is it?

What if what we consider to be fact is, in truth, fiction, and vice versa?

If we look at history, we see clearly that what was once accepted as "fact" (i.e., the world is flat) is now fiction.

Are we so prideful that we believe that the "truths" of modern science will not be disproved in the future? It would seem more sensible to look to history and realize that what is now "fact" might, in time, seem as ridiculous as the belief that the earth is the center of the universe. And yet, not many of us want to believe that we might still be living in the dark ages...

Why is this so?

Scientific discovery or *fact* eventually enters the cultural belief system and changes the definition of everything that culture perceives. After a while, the perception of the individuals who create culture actually changes to fit the "facts" of the time. We perceive what we are taught, and those perceptions create the world we live in.

Even those who continue to fight against the new definition—as in the case of Creationists—are forced, at least, to revise their original definition or be considered fools.

(For example, even most staunch Creationists admit that a Biblical "Day" as perceived by God was longer than a "day" as perceived by man. After all, the sun and moon weren't around to mark time before "the beginning.")

Once we have absorbed this new definition of reality, we feel content and secure, and tend to use it as a basis for other definitions or philosophies until a visionary breaks free of his learned perceptions and discovers a new way of perceiving reality. Then the process begins again and we are forced out of our comfort zone and must revise our reality systems once again.

Some definitions are more open to change than others. The discovery of viruses and germs were fairly easily absorbed by the culture. Subsequently, pasteurization became the vogue and doctors washed their hands more. Yet the discovery of molecular life didn't require us to really change our beliefs. Instead, such discoveries simply expanded our existing belief systems.

Definitions which do not disturb our fundamental beliefs—particularly those beliefs that give us a sense of security—are easily changed.

However, definitions which affect our values, our sense of worth, or our beliefs about order and safety are more difficult to change.

Darwin's theory of evolution which exiled man from the throne of Human-as-*un*animal and tossed him into the same evolutionary soup that the rest of the world's critters swim in, seemed almost like a fantasy, like Alice swimming with the other varmints in the Pool of Tears.

The theory of evolution was cause for the entire *scientific* community—not to mention those people who believed in the "divine" rights of man—to throw their arms in the air. But Darwin had it easy. He lived and even gained some popularity in his lifetime—unlike former scientific *heretics* like Copernicus and Galileo, or religious heretics such as Joan of Arc, Jesus and the millions of "witches" during the inquisition who were murdered or exiled. Remember the old warning never to discuss another man's politics or religion.

> In our current technological world, scientific and spiritual reality changes so quickly that no one is exempt from experiencing some form of anxiety.

We live in a veritable smorgasbord of realities! It is up to us to pick and choose which reality, belief system or religion to build our life on.

Freedom of choice is stressful, for when we have a choice, we can choose wrongly. Perhaps in this flood of realities, it's time that we build boats rather than houses. We must aim to **stay liquid** so we might flow through cataclysmic change without chronic anxiety. Otherwise, we'll end up sticking our heads in the sand like ostriches to avoid the stress of the exponential change of the times.

In our modern world even the operational definition of science has changed. It states that we can know what we can know and need not concern ourselves with things that we can't test at this time.

So, for science, the idea of a bearded God keeping records of all his creatures is meaningless because it cannot be tested.

(Although the *Noetic* Sciences are trying to find the God particle and prove that the numinous exists beyond or within "dead" matter, it is still a far cry from proof of a Personal God Who "loves" us.)

Of course, before we had instruments to detect the structure of the atom, we had no factual proof of atomic nature.

Yet, the idea of the atom or *prima materia* had a place in primitive cosmological theory, myth, religion and philosophy from the beginning of time.

As quantum scientists have pointed out, our whole definition of life is a fleeting construction and the ground of our **reality is constantly changing**. To live according to this concept is the backbone of the authentic human. Reality is ALIVE!

The Uncertainty Principle in Quantum Physics attests that any result of any experiment is dependent on the instruments one uses to conduct that experiment. This doesn't make the results untrue or only tentatively incomplete.

As Heisenberg noted, "We can only know that we can never know."

However, just because we cannot KNOW something, does not mean we cannot *experience* it!

As much as we desire some sort of proof or ground, we will be filled with anxiety. Our "definitions" of reality continue to change as we improve the technology we use to investigate such reality. An electron is both a wave and a particle. Schrodinger's cat is both dead and alive. However, most of this *apparent* confusion is a result of our language and categories.

This chaotic and open vision of science was so upsetting that Einstein could not agree to it. Einstein's belief system would not expand enough to embrace the idea that the universe often *appears* as a random game of dice. His belief in God was too strong. **But we must remember that the theory of randomness is also but a *theory*.** Like other belief systems, modern scientific theories fall into the category of metaphysics. Quantum physics is just newer and, therefore, seems more plausible than outdated theories—

such as a bearded God sitting on a throne in the clouds and hell as a place in the core of the earth.

Aldous Huxley makes this point in his discussion of the constellation Orion. With the naked eye, we see a "small faint smudge." Huxley tells us that many a grandiose cosmological philosophy was constructed from this smudge.

Yet however brilliant or complex a theory might be, it can never provide the same information that is gained through direct observation by a powerful "telescope, camera and spectroscope." The simple point of his argument is that information, knowledge and know-how disrupts and forces us to discard or, at least revise, former definitions, no matter how much we hate to do so. We are die-hard dogmatic romantics.

Wisdom—which is knowledge married with experience—is the key to cleansing "the doors of perception"...although it is not always pleasurable to pluck out the motes and splinters.

(For example, even religious folk might now consider that the story of Adam and Eve and the eating of the infamous Apple is actually a metaphor for the necessity of widening one's definitions through experience. A "fortunate Fall"!)

As we gather more information, many of us are required to change our belief systems. Some folk can do this easily while others have a hard time of it.

Since modern life IS ever-changing, if we strive for HAPPINESS, we need to alleviate the stress of change. To do this, **we must realize that "truth" (as defined by science) or "logic" is not as important as our need for meaning and purpose**.

However, OVER-attachment to the quest for MEANING can also keep us stuck. We must strive to experience life without the filters of past or present. In other words, to experience life as an Authentic Human.

Claiming the Burden of Wings

Lily Tomlin plays the character of an extraordinary homeless woman in the film *The Search for Intelligent Life in the Universe*. Her character tells the audience, "If you do only one thing with your life, evolve."

Changing your self and concurrently your perspective of the world is the most exciting thing you can do. (Although it can be devastating if such changes are imposed upon you rather than chosen by you.)

The more you change, the richer your life will be when you reflect upon it. The work and choice required if you are to claim the freedom to change is the core of the idea that freedom is a burden. Yet life, love, holidays, children, friends and beliefs are also burdens...and fun...aren't they?

Change requires an awareness of alternatives, along with the ability to make choices. While most of us have some limitations—whether financial, health or family—as long as we own our own minds, we have alternatives.

Our freedom to alter our future is contingent upon the depth of our consciousness and our willingness to incorporate new discoveries into our identity, desires and belief systems. We do not necessarily need to throw past discoveries out the window. Rather we can embrace a Both/And universe, an expansive universe, which expands to incorporate the new.

WHAT IN THE WORLD IS THE WORLD MADE OF?

Language, of course, is not limited to words, but includes images, feelings, movements, etc. Language also includes the code of your DNA and the binary code of your personal computer. Creative people acknowledge that language—by its structure—both restricts and allows change into the field of play. There is something to the fairy tale idea of magic words which open doors to new worlds. With language we can play out our intentions on the field. And we can also restrict them.

Yet language is a living entity, a mutable multitudinous being who is able to shapeshift into something of a trickster god. In fact, many of the trickster gods of mythology, such as Hermes, Thoth, Mercury and Legba, serve also as gods of language and communication.

Language can both make reality and mask it. Those interested in becoming their own masters will take pains to attack verbal dogmas while acknowledging language's innate power to transform the world. Plainly, the words you use—particularly those which you use habitually and unconsciously—will influence your reality.

There is a Zen story which illustrates the power of language to transform reality:

Once there was a terminally ill man who was being cared for by his family. They'd given up hope for a cure and were trying to make the last months of his life as comfortable as possible.

A Zen master visited the town. In a final effort, the sick man's family brought the man before the master. They asked the master to heal the man. The master then whispered a few words to the sick man and announced that soon the man would be well.

The brother of the sick man was skeptical because he knew how severe the illness was. He became angry that the Zen master would give false hope to his brother and confronted him. "Why are you giving my brother such false hopes?" he asked. "How can you heal him with only a few words?"

The master replied, "You know nothing of what goes on. You are simply an ignorant fool!" At this, the man's face turned red, and he lifted his hand to strike the master. The master, however, caught the man's hand and said, "Wait. Look at what change a few unkind words from me could bring about in you. If a few unkind words can change you so greatly, could not a few kind words bring healing to your brother?"

TIME IS THE MOTHER OF MANY WORLDS

New ideas often take many generations to affect the reality of the masses because of the time-binding qualities of language. It takes time for new discoveries to inform "the general tension and meaning of the time."

The information of the past informs and mis-informs—generation after generation.

New discoveries grow out of old discoveries—sometimes out of discoveries which eventually are proved to have no basis in reality.

For example, many now believe that Freud's model of psychology is a complete fiction. Nonetheless, Jungian theory—*which grew out of Freudian theory*—has become a separate model because we have labeled it with the term "Jungian" and have thus separated it from its source. So, even though Jungian theory derived from the "outdated" Freudian theory, we haven't re-evaluated it (yet).

The language we employ when describing our world affects the way we perceive our world. Most of us still describe the sun as "rising" and "setting," thus maintaining a medieval viewpoint of an anthropocentric universe.

> Exercise: Try describing the progression of the day as the Earth turning, rather than as the sun rising and setting, and see how it changes your perceptions.

The time-binding qualities of language aid humans to build on the past while giving us a common ground of reality, yet it also keeps our perceptions limited by the filters of the past, thus limiting our vision.

As an example, let's look at hypnosis. Many still believe that hypnosis is either the work of the "devil" or merely entertainment, and that it is neither useful nor open to scientific investigation.

Others maintain that hypnosis is useful to quit smoking or lose weight, but that using it as a substitute for chemical anesthesia in major surgery is not possible. They say, "How can words affect the body so it does not feel pain or heals faster, let alone communicate with the operation of cells."

ARE WORDS AND THOUGHTS REALLY POWERFUL ENOUGH TO HEAL YOUR BODY?

It is difficult for most of us to imagine that language (defined as words, thoughts or images) can dramatically affect how and what we feel and experience. Why? Because our belief system is limited by *our definition of matter*. Most of us still believe that matter cannot be changed with something as intangible as language, thoughts or beliefs.

Even though science has proved that matter is active and constantly changing, we perceive it as we were taught to perceive it—as solid. It is difficult for us to believe that hypnosis or Neuro-Linguistic Programming can affect something as "solid" as matter.

In fact, it is hard to believe that air is matter because we can't see, smell, hear, taste or touch it. In fact, before the Age of Enlightenment, many were under the illusion that the atmosphere was a spiritual substance called Ether.

Most of us believe that material things can only be directly experienced by our senses. Yet we all know that an Aboriginal Shaman perceives matter differently than a Midwestern American.

Alfred Korzybski—scientist, general semanticist and philosopher—pointed out that most individuals *automatically confuse the words they employ to describe things with the things themselves.* "The map is not the territory." This idea of Korzybski's is paramount in understanding our reality.

For instance, while we can take for granted that you aren't foolish enough to try to drink the word "water," remember that countless wars have been fought over words such as "freedom," "liberty" and "God"—words which hold different meanings for each individual.

In fighting for freedom, one easily forgets what freedom actually "is" and fights for *the word.*

Consider that two opposing armies may fight each other to the death for this abstraction labeled "freedom."

One army may be fighting for freedom *from* something, while the other is fighting for freedom *against* something, or freedom *to do* something, or freedom *not* to do something.

Do you think that the soldiers who are dying are fighting for freedom to die or freedom from pain? What does freedom mean to you?

> Stop right now and write down ten things you want freedom from, ten things you want freedom against, and ten things you want the freedom to (do).

Ponder this Question: Does language alter the way we perceive our world? If there were no word to describe "freedom" would you have bought this book in an effort to attain relatively more of it? If there was no word for food would you starve to death?

Do you agree or disagree with Korzybski's position that the use of the "is of identity" causes a great deal of trouble?

WORDS AND WORDS ONLY?

Korzybski posited that words probably have a reality structure of their own which no doubt significantly distorts the reality of what they refer to.

> Men argue over *concepts*, not over what the concepts refer to.

Who *owns* the water becomes more important than whether the water is good to drink.

Korzybski points out that the only way to understand what a word or concept means is to ask its user to tell you how it is similar to and how it is different from what it refers.

People react to certain words like Pavlov's dogs react to a bell. Certain words or phrases trigger certain emotional responses, depending on that person's past experience. Some words or phrases, such as those in newspaper headlines or advertisements, are purposely designed to trigger the emotions of an entire demographic or society. This is why marketers will always decide on the target demographic of a particular product before conceiving the appropriate language or imagery to sell that product.

An international video game company decided that their consumer service representatives must never use words like kill, die or death when referring to any violent action of any particular game.

If a consumer service representative is referring to an action where the animated character slices off the head of his opponent with a karate chop, he must use terms such as "defeat" or "finish" instead of "kill."

Soon, kids and adults alike will be thinking that decapitating does not mean killing someone (a bad thing), but rather means defeating the enemy (a good thing).

This form of brain-dirtying is highly effective. **How much different are we from Pavlov's dogs who salivate when a light comes on?**

The association of any particular image with a word works as an imprinting technique which facilitates learning. Many studies in language assimilation—particularly in students who are learning a second language—have found that image/word immersion techniques work on a far deeper level than consciously studying grammar or syntax.

These same studies have found that students assimilate material faster when they are relaxed and entertained, and not under the stress produced by formal learning situations. Students, particularly younger children, seem to pick up language subconsciously when they are exposed to it through image/word games.

While this may be good news for teachers in public schools, the implications of millions of young children assimilating information which associates *killing with winning* is disturbing.

Of course, such euphemistic talk has been employed by politicians and military officials for many years...

EXERCISE

Can you think of any dangerous euphemisms Hitler used to convince people that his concepts were useful to them?

How does your own government do the same?

Does advertising for the military promote the ideas of excitement and honor while ignoring the brutality and ugliness of war and death?

THE TRANCE IS OVER WHEN THE MUSIC STOPS

"Stop the World"

— Don Juan

Another example of *Word Trance* occurs when we attempt to place people in categories. We do this to make sense of the world we live in, but categorizing and defining objects and people, including ourselves, can be both limiting and painful.

Bumper sticker watchers might have noticed the increasing number of cars proclaiming the order "Kill Your Television."

Watching television has, in some circles, become classified as politically incorrect, if not an evil activity. Thus some people have put TV watching into the "bad" category. But is watching *all* television bad for the soul? Are *all* TV programs mind-dulling?

Perhaps the answer is not to kill your TV, but to learn to choose consciously what you watch. The TV is a tool which can be used to serve the awakening of the human potential as well as to keep the masses robotically purchasing useless items.

Similarly, in describing people, ask yourself if anyone is either *absolutely* selfish or *absolutely* altruistic? If you observe people in their natural setting you will notice "selfish people" being helpful and "helpful people" being selfish.

Categories are simply tools. They can be useful and they can be dangerous.

Think of terms like legal/illegal (sometimes only a jury or judge can tell; and it can depend on what state or country you're in).

Or consider sane/insane. William Blake, Salvador Dali, Ludwig van Beethoven, Alexander the Great, and many other "great" historical figures are now being labeled "bipolar" (formerly known as "manic-depressive")! In fact, a recent newspaper article attested to the fact that many contemporary high-ranking government officials were diagnosed as suffering from manic-depressive disorders.

To ascribe a definition to yourself or another is akin to creating a mental jail with words.

Think of all the great geniuses who would have been committed if they had thought themselves to be "insane" rather than "artistic" or "before their time," etc. Think of all the lives which would have been saved if men and women didn't ascribe definitions to particular groups like Jews, Blacks, Women, Witches, etc.

As Korzybski noted, **"Definitions which apply to everyone apply to no one."**

STAY LIQUID!

Try This

The next time a new acquaintance asks you the ubiquitous question, "What do you do?" consider your answer.

Are you just a writer, a grocery clerk, an artist, a computer programmer? Is that all you do? Do you really want that person to think of you primarily as that? And, more importantly, is your definition of what you do keeping you from doing what you dream to do? Has that decision to "be" a writer kept you from "becoming" a dancer? Is Baryshnikov a ballet dancer or a shopper when he's loading up his cart with Twinkies?

CAUSE AND EFFECT & THE CASE OF COLD SUSAN

The brain constantly searches for relationships as we observe the world. These relationships include "interactions," "correlations" and, quite often, "cause and effect." Most of us have brains which do this habitually in an effort to gain a sense of control over our lives.

We want the world to behave as we expect it to behave.

And most of us find it difficult and frightening to *respond* to the world, moment by moment: To Live In The Present. Or, as Ram Dass said, BE HERE NOW.

To enhance our sense of security, we manufacture causes or reasons for what happens in our lives.

Yet we often overlook certain elements of reality to create a cause which is in keeping with our individual belief systems.

For example, a Christian might tell herself that God is punishing her for SIN when life throws a punch, while a Hindu might tell himself that he is suffering because he was a bad person in a past life.

Sometimes, in an effort to make sense of our personal experiences, we will INVENT causes even if there IS NO CAUSE.

Consider the case of "Cold" Susan.

Susan is rushed to the hospital, unconscious from ingesting over 40 Valium. She had been despondent for three weeks after breaking up with her boyfriend.

The doctors pump her stomach and give her drugs to counteract the Valium. After a few days she is well enough to discuss her feelings with her doctor. Her boyfriend left her because he was not satisfied with their sexual relationship. He blamed Susan and labeled her frigid.

Then Susan's mother arrives. Susan refuses to see her, blaming her for the loss of the man she loved. Her mother becomes hysterical. She finds the doctor and asks him what's wrong with her daughter. The doctor says she is severely depressed and requires treatment.

He informs the mother that after extensive psychological and physical examinations a treatment plan will be designed to help Susan.

After a few more days the test results come back. They show some abnormalities in Susan's blood which indicate a hormonal imbalance. Susan's mother is relieved because, in HER MIND, this means that Susan is mentally healthy and she cannot be blamed for the way she raised her daughter. The problem is Susan's body, not Susan's self-esteem or the way she was brought up.

Susan is relieved because a hormonal dysfunction indicates that she is not "frigid"; she is simply suffering from a chemical imbalance.

The doctor gives Susan a prescription and refers her to another doctor on an outpatient basis for monitoring.

Three months pass and the follow-up tests no longer indicate a hormonal imbalance. Susan has been cured. She is no longer depressed. Everyone is happy. Susan simply had a hormonal imbalance which caused her frigidity, which in turn made her boyfriend leave her, which in turn caused her to attempt suicide.

(Do you believe the conclusions that Susan, her mother and doctors drew? While their conclusions *might* be true, there is no evidence to suggest a *correlation*, much less a *causal* relationship between the hormone imbalance and Susan's suicide attempt.)

Two months later Susan enters another relationship and her new boyfriend starts complaining about her sexual coldness.

This time Susan returns to the doctor and finds out that her hormones are out of balance again. He re-institutes hormonal therapy. Her boyfriend agrees to stay until the treatment takes effect. After a month Susan's hormonal level is back to normal, but there is no improvement in her sexual behavior. The doctor suggests that Susan seek psychotherapy. Both Susan and her mother strongly resist this advice.

Finally, Susan capitulates and enters Freudian analysis. After three years of analysis Susan is still "frigid."

Susan and her mother conclude that therapy is a waste of time, and that the problem resides in the way men behave sexually. They buy books on how men don't understand women. They conclude that what Susan needs is a "good" man who will respect and honor her.

We can see that everyone involved with Susan's case was more concerned about serving their own beliefs than helping Susan find love and happiness. (And, truthfully, most doctors do try to fit their patients' illnesses into their belief systems, which differ depending on which school of thought or medicine that the doctor studied.)

The mother didn't want to believe that her attitudes about sex and the way she raised Susan might be the problem. It was Susan's body that was at fault.

Susan didn't want to believe that she was frigid. There was something wrong with her body, and that was not her fault.

The doctor found a chemical imbalance and, as a good physician, he was taught to treat chemical problems with chemicals.

The analyst believed that Susan's mind was the problem and insisted on treating Susan with a therapy which has shown little success in dealing with frigidity.

By the time Susan was 30, she and her mother concluded that the problem was men. This face-saving device worked until Susan attempted suicide a few years later. After she recovered, she was sent to a behaviorist who used behavior therapy and hypnosis to "cure" Susan.

This treatment worked. Susan's fear of sexual contact no longer lead to a fearful reaction with her latest lover.

Everyone now concluded that Susan's problem was behavioral because it was "cured" by behavior therapy. (By the way, no one bothered to test Susan's hormonal balance until two years later when she was pregnant. They found that it was still out of balance.)

So what really was the cause of Susan's problem?

No one ever found out.

Just Because...

Warning: ANY absolute explanation for an affect—regardless of the definition of the former or the latter—may promote delusion, tight-mindedness and metaphysical constipation.

As long as the human species has been on the planet, "cause and effect" has been the great bug-a-boo for religion, philosophy and science. The activity of finding, or creating, a cause for any given effect adds much confusion to the world mainly because different belief systems promote different causes.

A Hindu—who believes in past-life Karma—will state a very different cause for the death of a child by starvation than will a Marxist.

Yet cause and effect are essential concepts in man's need to find meaning and control in his life.

Nietzsche, frequently called by other philosophers the "last metaphysician," says of cause and effect:

> ...'Explanation' is what we call it, but it is 'description' that distinguishes us from the older stages of knowledge and science. Our descriptions are better—but we do not explain any more than our predecessors. We have uncovered a manifold one-after-another where the naive man and inquirer of older cultures saw only two separate things. 'Cause' and 'effect' is what one says; but we have merely perfected the image of becoming without reaching beyond the image or behind it.
>
> ...In every chemical process, for example, quality appears as a 'miracle,' as ever; also, every locomotion; nobody has 'explained' a push. But how could we possibly explain anything? We operate only with things that do not exist: lines, planes, bodies, atoms, divisible time spans, divisible spaces. How could explanations be at all possible when we first turn everything into an *image*, our image!

Nietzsche felt that science simply allows us to describe ourselves "more and more precisely." He concludes this discussion of cause and effect by saying:

> ...An intellect that could see cause and effect as a continuum and a flux and not, as we do, in terms of an arbitrary division and dismemberment, would repudiate the concept of cause and effect and deny all conditionality.

Sounds very Zen, doesn't it?

We might also add that "an intellect that could see cause and effect as a continuum and a flux" is an intellect that has freed itself from the elusive quest for "why."

———◆———

There is a story about a man who sought to ask the Buddha questions about the meaning of life. He wanted to know whether the universe was eternal, whether the soul would survive the body, whether his life had any real meaning. He wanted an explanation of the universe and his place in it.

Buddha answered the man with a story:

"Suppose a man is wounded by a poisoned arrow and his family calls a surgeon to heal him. What if the man should say: 'I won't let this arrow be removed until I know who shot me, what his motive was, what he was wearing, what type of feather was on the arrow, who he bought it from, etc.?'"

If we focus entirely on finding the cause—the "why" of everything—we cease to *experience* life. *We may find ourselves on our deathbeds wondering where our lives have gone.*

So, while the arbitrary divisions we construct can be of aid to us in certain circumstances, they become veils which separate us from experiencing LIFE if we forget that they are, in fact, *constructs.*

One of the most pervasive constructs created by Western culture is the division of Mind and Body...

MIND VERSUS BODY

For the most part, Western Culture adheres to the belief system that body, mind and soul are separate entities.

Most Western religions put the soul on a pedestal. The body is to be overcome or mortified so that one's immortal soul can be redeemed.

During the age of enlightenment, the notion that "mind" (or reason) rather than "soul" holds precedence over the body was popularized. As Descartes famous tenet attests: "I think, therefore I am."[1] This dualistic belief is comforting to humans because it gives us hope that we will live on beyond the inevitable decay and death of the body. (However, such thinking *assumes* that the mind/soul will not decay like matter.)

Belief in an immortal mind or soul is a matter of faith. Because of the human habit to live in the future, rather than the present, we are constantly living in fear of death. As life hits us with the deaths of loved ones, we get stuck worrying about the future and find solace in the belief that the soul or mind outlives the body

It is soothing to think that the mind-soul will continue its existence in another world—preferably a better world. No wonder the tacit preference for the mind over body. Even the educated and intellectually enlightened hold the body in low regard.

Consequently, the care of individuals has been divided between those who heal the body, those who heal the soul, and those who heal the mind. If we catch the flu, we go to a physician; if we catch a demon, we see a priest; and if we catch a case of depression, we see a therapist.

No wonder one of the diseases spawned in modern times is an intense and painful feeling of alienation.

Most of us can attest to feeling dis-eased much of the time. Interestingly, the word "heal" stems from the Old English word for "whole." (This is not to say that we should resurrect the archaic idea that all disease is caused by demonic possession, or the scientific idea that all disease is completely physical, or the

---

[1] This, of course, has been turned on its head a million times: "I am, therefore I think."

New Age idea that all disease is mental and caused by negative thoughts. Absolutism can make you miserable!)

Life is confusing. When you feel dis-eased, should you go to the Freudian, the Jungian, the Rolfer, the Rebirther, the M.D., the priest, the rabbi, the professor, or just hope it goes away by itself before you die? Where are you going to get the money, not to mention the time?

The lists can go on and on.

It seems that humans have been carved into pieces giving each group something to work on. *Dividing a whole into parts is a convenient way to study how parts might work. But to believe that this division is real, simply because we have made an arbitrary division, is delusional.*

> This is the ultimate consequence of the power of words: Language creates realities, for better or worse.

As individuals, we also tend to classify things according to a basic scheme built into our language or linguistic grid.

We take such classifications for granted, forgetting that we have *learned* them somewhere (probably in grammar school) and that we have never really bothered to question their authority.

The schematic built into our language influences us to such a degree that most of the time we only see the things we can easily classify, while we overlook everything else.

Psychological tests have shown that when people from different cultures catalogue objects in a given picture, they will point out and "see" only those objects with which they are familiar. As Wendell Johnson said, "We see with our categories."

Exercise

Attempt to classify something differently from how you're used to. Attempt to classify your arm besides dividing it into fingers, hands, forearm, wrist, etc. Is there really a line dividing your wrist from your hand?

TIME TO REGROUP

"Mind" and "body" are simply words we employ so we can figure ourselves out. We've lost sight of the fact that mind and body are arbitrary divisions of a whole system. We have deluded ourselves into thinking and acting as if "body" and "mind" exist as independent physical entities, with the latter outliving the former. Every "body" healer also affects the mind and every "mind" healer affects the body.

Likewise, we believe the system of our mind-bodies is separate from our environments. In nature, there is no such thing as a solitary person. There is no such thing as an environment independent of the person in it. "Mind," "body" and "environment" are simply words which refers to aspects of a whole system.

When we allow ourselves to become imprisoned by our categories, we cease to perceive the continuum of life and fall into a rut of alienation.

Thich Nhat Hanh tells us that we must learn to *see as a poet sees,* or as one who sees *beyond* what s/he has learned to see or expects to see:

> If you are a poet, you will see clearly that there is a cloud floating in this sheet of paper. Without a cloud there will be no water; without water, the trees cannot grow; and without trees, you cannot make paper.
>
> So the cloud is in here.
>
> The existence of this page is dependent on the existence of a cloud.
>
> Paper and cloud are so close.
>
> Let us think of other things, like sunshine.
>
> Sunshine is very important because the forest cannot grow without sunshine, and we humans cannot grow without sunshine. So the logger needs sunshine in order to cut the tree, and the tree needs sunshine in order to be a tree. Therefore you can see sunshine in this sheet of paper.
>
> And if you look more deeply, with the eyes of a bodhisattva, with the eyes of those who are awake, you see not only the cloud and the sunshine in it, but that everything is here: The wheat that became the bread for the logger to eat, the logger's father—everything is in this sheet of paper.

AT PLAY IN THE FIELD OF LIES

Perceiving mind and body as interdependent systems has been called psychophysical parallelism in some scientific circles. (So-called "primitive" peoples may call it "living.") Psychophysical parallelism means that what happens in the "mind" simultaneously happens in the "body." Conversely, what happens in the "body" happens in the "mind." What this implies is that the mind/body/soul distinction might just be WRONG!!!

UH-OH! The foundation of our entire Western civilization may be crumbling. As Chicken Little said, "The Sky is Falling!" Or could it be that we are beginning to See the Sky Clearly, now that the clouds are fading away?

One common argument for the interdependence of body, mind and soul shows how illness is affected by belief, hope, desire, success or failure. It has been noted by many an M.D. that the immune system seems to be strengthened by positive thinking, while compromised by chronic anxiety.

Attitude affects how we feel, and how we feel affects our attitude. However, any concept can be taken to an extreme. Religions such as Christian Science have evolved from the belief that "mind" and "body" are connected into a dogmatic belief that "mind" controls "body."

Whereas traditional Western medicine has ignored the interconnectedness of mind, soul and body—with the result that disease was exiled into the realm of body alone—some practitioners of Christian Science have gone the other way and denied the intelligence of the body.

Many a child has died because a Christian Scientist has refused to employ the assistance of drugs or surgery while insisting that the mind, by the power of prayer, is the only proper medicine.

The preference for "mind" theories over "body" theories stems from cultural beliefs which presuppose that mind is free and godlike, while body is a machine.

This is similar to the beliefs of the Deists who thought of the world itself as a mechanical structure which could be wholly known and controlled if one just had enough information.

As previously mentioned, the concept that mind is separate from body is particularly comforting as we watch our bodies decay and confront the inevitability of death.

———◆———

Earlier we discussed Pribram's theory which states that our present perceptions are influenced by our past experiences.

His experiments imply that subjective, so-called "immaterial experiences" affect and change brain structure and, at the same time, the new brain structures alter any subjective experience.

More recently, studies utilizing CAT scans of the brains of Buddhist monks have shown that the pleasure areas of the brains light up when the monks chant. Even the act of smiling—forced or not—causes the brain to release endorphins, the chemicals of pleasure.

Can we actually sing and smile ourselves into a state of Bliss?

Reality depends on the eye or ear or nose or hand or tongue or mood that beholds it.

The instrument we use to measure "reality" is our brain and, as Heisenberg pointed out, an instrument affects the outcome of any experiment.

Our instruments—sense organs, brain, nerves, etc.—are inextricably tied up with that thing we love to hate: our body.

Pribram's theory threatens dualistic thinking since even the most staunch dualist has to admit that the physical brain is part of the body, even if he continues to insist that the mind/soul exists beyond the lifespan of the body.

Man is an organism oscillating between chronic discontent and tranquil belief. For every "truth" invented to comfort us, an opposite "truth" emerges which sooner or later elicits doubt. Living in a state of constant doubt can be PAINFUL!

And yet, philosophers and spiritual leaders continue to create and invent truths that give us a degree of security, or rather, that help humans cope with their fear of the future. Why not just think about being PRESENT?

We consider ourselves "modern." We laugh at the idea that the world was once considered flat or that a bunch of gods on Mount

Olympus played with our lives. But these falsities kept us sane and, like our modern lies, are hard to jettison.

From amidst this myriad of error we have survived again to stick our heads out of the mud to see the sun heralding a new day—only to stick it back into the mud time and time again.

Of course, a mud bath *is* soothing to the skin. Perhaps we must learn to play in truths, enjoy them as a grand illusion of human life, without adhering to them or allowing them to keep us from growing.

PART II

THE PRACTICE OF PUTTING YOURSELF ON

THE PSYCHO-PHYSICAL JOURNEY

Have you felt the joy of the sun warm your skin after a long winter? No doubt you can recall that sensation by imagining yourself in that circumstance. If 100 people tried this exercise, each would remember a different set of images to help them to re-experience the sensation.

Some might acknowledge this fact by nodding their head. Others will need to say "yes" to themselves, while still others need do nothing.

Each of us has a personal style of relating, remembering, thinking and living. And at one time or another each of us has changed our style to suit the needs and desires of our present situation.

Many of us seek to change our style of relating with the world consciously—and work very hard to do so—utilizing means such as therapy, self-help books and willpower. It is safe to say that we all have used our own creative urges to enhance and improve our life situations at one time or another.

If you would like to improve your style of relating to life, loved ones, and learn what brings you happiness in the here-and-now, then the following exercises will be of use to you.

If you simply want to learn the root of why you continue to do things that frequently sabotage you, the exercises in this book can help you root out those painful feelings which are hidden away in the dark closets of your mind.

STOP! DO THIS:

Before beginning the Psycho-Physical Journey, create a place of sanctuary for yourself. You may want to curl your body into a comfortable position, or light incense or candles to create a safe space. Take the phone off the hook. Create a space where you are free to express yourself without inhibition. There is no need to fix what you think is broken or strive to become enlightened or judge yourself.

During our Psycho-Physical journey you will be asked to perform certain tasks, but before we reach that point it is important for you to understand what Psycho-Physics really is.

At Play in the Transactional Fields

or: Becoming a God

Psycho-Physics concerns the relationship between mind-soul and body. Every mental action has a physical consequence and every physical action has a mental consequence. The Mind-Soul-Body is an interconnected system.

Think about how each cell in your body contains the genetic information of the whole you.

The idea that the mind-soul is separate from the physical body defies common sense if you take into consideration that the mind grows from the body. As William Blake wrote in his prophetic masterpiece *The Marriage of Heaven and Hell*:

> Man has no Body distinct from his Soul, and that called Body is a portion of Soul discerned by the five Senses, the chief inlets of Soul in this age.

Beyond Psycho-Physics there is the relationship between person and environment. Every environment affects the person; every personal act affects the environment. If you grew up with unloving parents, you know that when you visit your parents' home, you will feel dis-eased for that environment will affect you. A supportive, loving environment, whether it be people or nature, might make you feel free and happy. To separate environment from person is impossible. Environment affects our perception and our reality. This is why every being's reality is liquid!

It is not that a "true" "reality" does not exist—it may or may not—but *talking* about any reality other than a *perceived reality* is meaningless. The reality which any of us can grasp is transactional: *the perceiver shapes the external world according to his or her cultural, personal, religious and genetic bias.*

The concept of who you are at any given moment does not exist except in relation to the given environment.

It is essential to realize that your reality is based on who you are at PRESENT...if you are dissatisfied with your self and your circumstances, and you truly wish to change your life!

Don't worry! The absence of One Solid Reality does not need to be feared. You are not falling into an abyss. Neither is this concept akin to nihilism. What the absence of One Solid Reality allows is **Play**.

As the philosophical school of post-structuralism pointed out, once you get rid of the limiting metaphysical structures you learned during your life (whether a punishing God, Hell, Karma, etc.), you set yourself free to play on infinite fields.

Life As an Alchemical Process

Our mind-brain develops over time and contains many associations which have developed through learning. **Learning itself is a type of alchemical process which changes the learner.**

We are very conscious of some associations. For instance, when we hear the word "water" most of us will either imagine some kind of water or look around for some water. We know that the mouth-sound "water" refers to a wet substance that is good to drink, swim in or wash with. Other associations may be less obvious to us even though they may influence our reactions to stimuli.

Complex associations of the unconscious kind were often created during times when the critical-analytical part of the mind was not capable of differentiation or evaluation (e.g., when we were either too young to think). Thus, any type of cortical intervention into the automatic reactions we learned is difficult (and perhaps impossible), to restructure.

How can we change our habits if we don't know the why, how or when of how we got them? We try to change ourselves by willpower, yet willpower does not effect permanent changes and usually we end up the same as before—or worse. (Just think about the results of your last diet or talk to anyone who has attended Alcoholics Anonymous.)

What and how we learn is fundamentally dependent on the neuro-biochemical state of the learner at the time of the learning experience. During peak experiences—such as our first sexual experience or the birth process—the actual chemical state of the learner is more *receptive* to what might be called psycho-physical programming.

This programming often becomes an automatic, reactive process causing us to repeat the same self-defeating habits.

As Ralph Waldo Emerson said, "Our faith comes in moments, but our vice is habitual."

(Here, the word "faith" does not mean blind belief, but refers to a feeling of interconnectedness with life and Universe. In fact the Buddhist word for faith, *sraddha*, literally means "to put one's heart on." It's etymologically similar to the Latin *cor* from which the words "heart" and "courage" are derived.)

We find the most obvious and clear example of automatic reactive process in cases of traumatic amnesia. Here, the person in his normal state cannot recall the events of the trauma yet his or her reactions to stimuli are obviously affected by such trauma.

This occurs in many victims of child abuse. As adults, these people do not recall being abused, yet they suffer from the inability to relate, trust or achieve intimacy in relationships. They often react inappropriately, yet seem helpless to do anything about their reactions. This is because they aren't sure what *triggered* their reaction. It often feels as if they were on auto-pilot, which is actually correct because the body remembers the trauma which the mind has blanked out.

If, for example, a child experienced a trauma in which he learned subconsciously to associate heights with life-threatening danger, as an adult he may find himself reacting to heights even in safe circumstances, with physical symptoms of sweating, vertigo and irrational tantrums.

Sometimes a simple word can trigger a reaction. Suppose a child associated the word "brat" with feelings of abandonment. If a potential mate calls that grown-up child a brat, even teasingly, she may suddenly decide that the relationship is no good, without ever acknowledging the real reason her feelings changed.

Under hypnosis, the events and resulting emotions are often clearly experienced and expressed. Once the trauma is named, the awareness of *why* the person reacts in self-defeating manners can be better addressed and, through work, overcome.

A less obvious, but more common example of this intriguing psychophysical relationship is the day-to-day "loss" of memory which is often due to changes in bio-psychological rhythms. Some psychologists have called this "state-dependent learning."

How many times have you had a certain name or word on the "tip of your tongue" only to finally remember it when the moment of need is long gone? When the memory "pops" in again it is usually due to the replication of the bio-psychological state in which the information was learned. Criminal psychologists (and TV detectives) often reconstruct the scene of a crime to "jar" the victim or witness into remembering details about what happened—details which had previously been forgotten.

A Lot of It *Is* in the Name

When a traumatic set of events have occurred, the Mind-Body develops a behavior to cope with these events. But this does not mean that you must remain victimized by either the painful experience or the adaptive behavior used to cope with the situation. Instead, you can become conscious of the behavior, feel the pain, and let go of any habits which have ceased to serve you.

The key to removing painful or non-useful behavior and emotional states is to acknowledge the experiences encoded at a deeper level, bring them to light, and restructure them. In other words, change the inside to change the outside!

To name something is to assert a kind of power over it. Magicians believed that the name of a thing was a sort of spiritual handle by which the thing itself could be manipulated. The word "poet" stems from the Greek word *poiein*, which means to create. The poet, of course, was a namer of things and, thus, a creator.

Restructuring behavior patterns necessitates both creation and destruction. We can not destroy non-useful patterns until we admit that we are trapped by such behaviors, and decide to destroy them.

I (Hyatt) will use myself as an example. As a child I was publicly compared to a relative who everyone claimed was more intelligent than I was. When I was placed into a learning situation, the anxiety I experienced from fearing that I would not be able to prove that I was at least as intelligent as this relative slowed my ability to retain and recall information. Therefore I, and everyone else, believed I was stupid—since it is assumed that intelligence is reflected by the ability to memorize, recall and verbalize information.

I frequently failed at "tests" of intelligence and dropped out of school at the age of 16. If you were to review my grades you would note that I was a D+ to C- student although my IQ scores were above normal.

I joined the Navy at 17 and on the first exam, I scored the highest. My Chief Petty Officer stated that he couldn't believe it was me, and that I must have cheated. Thereafter, I never scored above a C again.

After I left the Navy I took the High School GED. Not only did I pass, but I received 18 college units which included such subjects as chemistry, physics, English, math, social science and psychology. Not only had I received low scores in these subjects while in school, I never even finished the last two years of high school. While I was not able to verbalize the information I had learned while in High School, I obviously had learned something! The information was there, but I couldn't access it because I subconsciously had learned that I was too stupid to learn. I BECAME what I was TOLD I was!

This brief history demonstrates that learning did take place at some level and was, in fact, encoded in my mind-body. My inability to recall information was due to the chronic tension that I felt when I was put on the spot, which in turn was due to the self-defeating, automatic behavior pattern caused by my family's insistence that I was inferior to my relative.

The effect of this anxiety (read: non-useful information) interfered with my ability to recall and verbalize my knowledge while in the environment of a classroom.

When I was placed in a different learning situation—that of taking an exam with strangers who would not judge me—my anxiety lessened and I could access the information and write it down. Yet, I couldn't recall the same information verbally and publicly five minutes after the exam. When my friends asked me about the questions on the exam I couldn't remember even one. I had a form of amnesia.

While you may not have had an experience like mine, I am sure that you have had similar experiences where an emotional state either interfered with or elicited information.

Breaking the Bonds of Fear

Fear and anxiety are learned habits created during times when the critical-evaluative mind did not have the ability to interfere with the creation of a "biochemical-neural bond" (BCNB).

Some behavioral scientists have called these responses "conditioned emotional reactions" (CER). While these bonds served a very useful purpose for survival in the context in which they were created, they usually end up causing pain and misery in our present environment. These behaviors, habits or emotive responses are often hindrances to our enjoyment of life and success.

Why it is so difficult to remove these bonds? It is because each bond is part of our whole nature. It has a biochemical and neural basis which has been strengthened by the fact that, at one time or another, it served a useful purpose, even if that purpose was only to please our mommy and daddy when we relied on them for survival.

Even though such behaviors cause pain, they are hard-wired in our body-minds because these habits and beliefs once protected us. They continue to hinder us until we figure out the cause and work it out of the physical, mental, spiritual and emotional aspects of ourselves.

As a recovering alcoholic said about his ten years of failing to stay on the wagon: "I always thought that getting drunk was a preferred alternative to suicide." As the man gained more awareness of why he drank to excess, he was able to gain some control over his life.

As he began to enjoy his life, the urge to commit suicide left him and he was able to kick the drinking habit which no longer served him. If he didn't drink at the time he did, he might have committed suicide and not had the opportunity to enjoy his life.

> Don't fall into the trap of feeling guilty for the sins of the past by labeling these bonds as "bad" or "evil."

The fact that biochemical-neural bonds cause much of your misery may make you feel depressed: it may seem like a big hunk of work to break a physical bond. You might say to yourself, "If this is true, how can we change such a biochemical-neural bond without the use of drugs. How can we replace non-useful behaviors with creative and more flexible survival strategies?"

Let me put your mind at ease. That some of our difficulties are due to biochemical-neural bonds is a most hopeful statement since the brain is always growing, re-evaluating and re-programming itself. **The brain is not fixed!** Anything which has been created can be changed if you simply know how.

The Authentic Human reminds us to STAY LIQUID!

Rejoice that the latest findings in brain research do not support the belief that an "old dog cannot learn new tricks." Past events which affect your behavior patterns today do not necessarily have to dictate your behavioral style in the future.

> Life will not cease to be challenging, but the past—your past—need not be a terminal condition.

External drugs are not essential for change to take place because the brain is a gigantic biochemical manufacturing plant!

YOUR BRAIN is your very own bio-pharmacy! *You* are the head pharmacist.

Runner's "high" is a well-known state of being in which the body goes into a sort of overdrive when the brain releases endorphins. High doses of cayenne pepper are also known to produce endorphins.

Mind-altering drugs, particularly psychedelic drugs, have been used by many cultures and movements to effect brain change. Psychotropic drugs—sometimes hailed as a kind of lazy man's way to enlightenment—work because they stimulate the release of endorphins, serotonin and other neuro-chemicals that already exist in your brain.

Terrence McKenna, an authority on the shamanistic use of psychotropic plants, joked that every human being alive could be arrested for possession of the illegal and powerful hallucinogenic DMA. Why? Because DMA naturally exists in our brains.

Many antidepressants work by increasing the neurotransmitter serotonin. These drugs, however, don't contain serotonin. Rather they block the re-uptake of serotonin by the pre-synaptic neurons, thereby causing the accumulation of serotonin, which is already being created in varying amounts in our brains.

The Habit of Fear

Franklin Delano Roosevelt said, "We have nothing to fear but fear itself." Aleister Crowley wrote, "Fear is failure, and the forerunner of failure." Smart men! Conquering fear is like slaying a dragon, and we are all called to be knights if we are to change our lives, and the lives of our planetary companions, for the better!

Most of the fears you are consciously or unconsciously feeding are probably causing you stress and preventing you from becoming the person you want to be. But it's nigh impossible to conquer your fears when you don't know what they are or why they continue to hang about your neck.

The 2010 film "Inception" deals with the power of ideas when implanted in the subconscious. The film's protagonist, Mr. Cobb, must acknowledge a past deed which led to the suicide of his wife, travel down into the basement of his subconscious, and *kill the idea* of his deceased spouse to rid himself of the guilt and shame that are ruining his life. Similarly, the heir of an empire, who consciously heard his father say "disappointed" on his deathbed, must enter the subconscious vault in his mind to realize that his father was not disappointed that his son was not following in his footsteps, but rather he was disappointed that his son tried so hard to be like him. In the depth of his subconscious, the heir remembers his father's last words, which were not of disapproval as he thought.

Like Mr. Cobb who might have committed suicide or gone insane if he "let go" of the idea that his wife was still alive in the subconscious cellar, his behavior was once useful.

Similarly, your fears continue to accompany you because they served you at one time. Because we fear CHANGE, we become comfortable with our fears. They are almost like an abusive lover you can't leave, for fear of the unknown. Worse, some of your fears resemble a *phantom* lover, acting like a silent succubus insidiously sucking your soul and life energy.

Even so, there's a part of yourself that's attached to this lover simply because it's something to hold onto. **Simply put, old pain is often more comfortable than the unknown.**

Thus, even painful and self-defeating fears can give you a sense of confidence because they are familiar. For example, when you were a child you might have feared thunder. You might have expressed this fear to your parents who subsequently let you cozy up nice and warm in bed with them.

From this you began to associate a fear of thunder with the comfort and safety of sleeping under the protective wings of parents. Though as an adult you may no longer indulge in the same ploys which worked as a child, the association of fears with protection may subconsciously be sabotaging your work, relationships and self-esteem.

Association of fear with comfort—which many of us learned via religion or unfortunate parenting or both—can sometimes lead us to chronically choose mates or bosses which block our ability to maximize our potential.

When we choose mates who constantly berate or even physically abuse us, we often stay in the relationship because of the subconscious association of fear with protection or survival, or simply feeling that we are loved, even if our spouse hits us. We may even go out of our way to "get a rise" out of a mate, to "prove" that we are loved. Obviously, in doing so we habitually sabotage our happiness.

Overcoming our fears is difficult because your *sense* of identity is as dependent on your fears as it is on your beliefs. We say "sense" of identity because your real identity is hard-wired by nature for the protection and maintenance of life. *Real* identity is prescribed by your DNA.

Once you realize that you can replace these restrictive, fearful survival strategies with useful, creative, expansive strategies, you can easily let go of them. As you rid yourself of fears and behavior patterns which are no longer useful, you will slowly discover a fundamental strength in yourself and others.

Underneath your *learned sense* of identity is a strong human being, a survivor, who seeks to live life to the fullest and to its utmost potential. In other words, you become an Authentic Human and live in the present, without constant anxiety, without limits, without crutches. CHOOSE LIFE!

A Smart Pig Can Recognize a Pearl When He Sees One

Consider this analogy: A person has a bad kidney. If he doesn't get it replaced, he will die or live a severely restricted life attached to a kidney machine.

A surgeon implants a donor kidney, yet the recipient's body rejects it. Why? Because it is foreign to the body. The healthy kidney literally begins to destroy itself, even though it is necessary for the recipient's survival.

To stop the body from destroying the new kidney, the physician gives the patient drugs which help the body adjust to it. The drugs fool the body into believing that the kidney is not alien, and reduce the rejection response. In time the body accepts the kidney, and the person goes on to live a healthy life.

In a similar way, new and healthier behaviors often feel foreign and alien at first. Even though you know that the new behavior patterns will help you reclaim your joy, you fall back into the old, non-useful habits. The new behaviors do not match the biochemical reality models that already exist in the brain. Remember, these structures are not just psychological, they include physical bonds with *real substance*.

If you don't acknowledge that the behavior patterns which you want to change or remove are physical as well as emotional and mental—if you rely on willpower to change those habits—you will find yourself falling off the wagon—again. However, if you acknowledge that any habit or behavior has a Body-Mind structure, you will find that, like any other physical substance, the behavior can be changed. All you need to know is what tools to use.

So don't be discouraged if at first your brain attempts to reject the new behavior. The brain is doing what it was designed to do, holding fast to habits and behaviors that helped it survive in the past. Your brain has a very good memory for learning tricks. The brain is so creative that it will attempt to prove that the dangers which were present when these behaviors were created still exist.

Those suffering from addiction, abusive circumstances, chronic pain, low self-esteem, fear of success, may be able to set themselves free. But it takes work! Contrary action is necessary. You may not feel like doing something, but work on facing each fear and soon new behaviors and habits will evolve. A feeling is just a feeling. It's up to you to become the meta-programmer of your brain and teach it new tricks.

The brain's ability to convince itself and its body that the dangers or situations which effected the construction of behavior patterns are at the root of what are commonly called "self-fulfilling prophecies."

Expecting a certain event to occur, we create the circumstances which will *make* that event occur. If we are run by behavior patterns and expectations which are restrictive and self-defeating, our life can become a series of catastrophes.

So how do we actually change? What most mind-therapists have missed is that it makes no sense—and, frankly, just doesn't work—to remove unacceptable behavior patterns without providing a new and better replacement along with the skill to use the new behavior. So, the first thing to do is uncover and acknowledge WHY you keep doing what you don't want to do (i.e., the subconscious roots of any self-defeating behavior). Then apply *contrary behavior*: That is, exchange the out-dated, self-defeating, painful, un-useful behavior with a new habit chosen by you that gives you pleasure, peace and joy!

Even if you don't feel like doing something different, *do it*. Act contrary to your habit. If you want to stop drinking four martinis to wind down after work, try exercising or walking instead, even if you *feel* exhausted. Begin to *act*, rather than *react* to your feelings. Acting contrary or opposite to your habitual, knee-jerk reactions will eventually help you conquer your habit and give you control over your responses. A response is much different than a reaction.

You (your brain and your body) must realize that what was once of use is being replaced with something better. It will give up an old behavior pattern much easier if it is given a more useful pattern in trade. Start with respecting your brain and your body.

Stop Now and Try This

Choose a behavior pattern or habit which does not serve you. As this is an exercise which will attempt to establish confidence, do not choose a habit or pattern which you've tried (unsuccessfully) to break in the past. Do not choose a habit which you are dependent on for emotional support or comfort (smoking, drinking or over-eating). Just choose a habit which doesn't serve you. Then choose a replacement habit; something which will serve a purpose or enhance your life in some way.

For instance, for this particular exercise I chose the simple, but non-useful pattern, of not brushing my teeth before going to bed as something I wanted to change. For a replacement pattern, I chose the creation of a dream diary. In order to write in the diary I had to brush my teeth.

Keep a record of whether or not you replaced the old behavior with the new one. Do not judge yourself or put yourself down if you slip up. Just continue to keep a record.

BREAKING UP IS HARD TO DO

Restructuring behaviors can be painful. Like divorcing an abusive spouse on whom you are dependent, you will often feel conflicted between comfortable security and fulfilling your potential and being happy.

It is easier to learn new skills which do not have a strong emotional impact. This is, perhaps, one reason why small children—who haven't as yet created a large number of behavioral bonds—learn so easily. They will jump on a bicycle and race down a hill confidently until they learn to associate speed with the emotional shame and physical pain of the crash.

If the child does not get back on the bike and prove to himself that speed does not necessarily mean crashing, he may go the rest of his life driving in a metaphorical slow lane.

Breaking up with old habits can be as emotional as breaking up with your lover. When any behavior pattern is associated with deep emotions—particularly fears and anxieties which were programmed into your software during times of extreme crisis—change is more difficult, particularly if you're not aware of why or when the behavior pattern was created and installed. Have you ever heard a newly divorced person say something like "I miss the fighting"?

Fortunately, over the past few decades researchers have learned much about how the brain and the nervous system operate and have developed new methods to help individuals use their creative resources to remove and replace behavior which is no longer useful or is hindering one's life.

Many therapists now believe that it is often unnecessary to dig into the deep resources of the psyche as is promoted by, for example, the Freudian schools of thought. This is good news for most of us since many traditional therapies are too lengthy and too costly for most people.

SELF-ASSESSMENT

To help you become a more powerful self-restructurer and bring out your potential, it is necessary to assess your present and latent strengths. Knowing what seeds are waiting in the soil helps the farmer cultivate those seeds into healthy, strong plants. It is important to assess your strong points and undeveloped potential every month or so in order to understand your progress. Doing this will give you a concrete sense of how to continue to develop your Self, while updating and changing your program when needed.

Start with the following exercise and remember: Stay Liquid!

Stop and Do It Again

Get a piece of paper and something to write with. Allow yourself to find your state of sanctuary, your safe place. From within that safe place begin to think about your strengths—what you've accomplished in life so far. Don't be afraid to list small achievements. No one is going to read this list but you. Take a few minutes to do this.

Next, let yourself fantasize: try to remember the dreams you had for yourself. Recognize your fantasy self—whether you see yourself as a rock star, a writer, or the head of the Illuminati—as a latent strength. Write down the strengths which you demonstrate when enacting a fantasy role. Are these strengths mirrored in your real life? Don't judge.

As you continue reading this book, jot down any strengths—present or latent—which pop into your head.

You Are the Artist That Paints Your Life

"Who is the Master who makes the Grass Green?"
— Zen Koan

During the self-assessment process, it will become increasingly clear that you have the power to reprogram your brain on many levels.

Moments of clarity should be taken seriously, even if you don't understand what these epiphanies mean. *Trust yourself.* Don't get bogged down trying to understand everything that you feel. Thinking too much is neither required nor suggested. Instead, journal for a few minutes every day. By writing down your feelings, not only will you learn how mutable feelings are, but also what triggers non-useful behavior. And, of course, you will be recording your progress. You will find as weeks go by that you really are changing!

Your progress toward owning your own life is not always linear, nor conscious. Your job is to go about your life while you perform the exercises, remaining confident that reprogramming your brain is often a non-linear process. Do the work and trust yourself!

Let go of your expectations. Remember that tension is the primary culprit. Fear and anxiety works like glue, bonding us to our past.

Realize that if you **change your environment, your environment will change you.** Any given reality is transactional. Plato viewed truth as the correspondence of the mind and environment. If you fill your mind (and imprint the body) with painful images or memories, you probably will end up believing the lie that life is painful. The perceiver plus the perceived environment results as The World As You Know It. "We are all greater artists than we realize," Friedrich Nietzsche wrote. And if your world is painful, perhaps it is time to end the world as you know it.

Remember: It is up to you whether you paint a nightmare or a work of beauty! But first you need to exhume the subconscious roots of un-useful behavior.

Of course, when you commence being a brain-change technician, you may also notice behaviors that could slow your progress. For example, if you find yourself acting like a control freak, the process of "Un-doing" yourself might bring you to your knees. Change is the friendly enemy of control freaks. If you *imagine* yourself as a victim, you will often *act* as victim and fall under a devastating spell cast by the greatest illusionist in your life: yourself.

You will put yourself into a self-destructive trance and believe the LIE that you are unable to change your circumstances. You will find yourself believing the LIE that you are trapped in misery because of your past.

To believe that you are trapped severs you from the world. You end up painting an imaginary (and hellish) barrier between your learned perception and Real LIFE! The magician's art is the practice of changing consciousness at will. This is not easy—particularly if you've been stuck in a state of depression or anxiety for years—but it is not impossible.

As a wise man once said, "Sometimes your house must burn to the ground before you can see the New Dawn!" Often it takes a torrent of tears to break the dam of your past.

Stop Now and Do It:
Crisis is Change!

It is no coincidence that the Chinese symbols for the word "crisis" are identical to those of "opportunity." They are literally translated: "Crisis is an opportunity riding the dangerous wind." Etymologically, crisis means *breaking apart*. But divorcing yourself from misery is a good thing! Work on doing things contrary to what you did in the past. This will give you confidence and help break away from habits and ruts!

TRY THIS: Imagine a time when you were in crisis. A time of grief or even one of euphoria. Both intense sorrow and euphoria create a state of crisis, wherein the shell of your self-concept is broken apart and revelation becomes available.

The hermetic aphorism tells us the secret of bliss: "In Laughter, Tears; In Tears, Laughter."

During times of crisis, tension is released and we are freed from fear. We are temporarily relieved of the bonds which enforce our habitual styles. This is why people sometimes find superhuman strength and energy during times of crisis. We surrender our separateness from the world and find ourselves totally in the present! Free!

Relax in your Sanctuary and use your imagination to visualize a time when you were in crisis. Let yourself feel the surrender. In this state you can—by working hard—create new and more useful ways of living.

Yet One More Reminder Before You Begin

Fact: How you experience the world (your REALITY) depends on your individual perception as filtered through your belief system, programming, etc., *combined* with any given environment in time-space.

If you wish, ask your deeper layers (i.e., INTUITION) to provide you with insights and progress reports from time to time. We will teach you how to do this, but remember it is not necessary unless it interests you.

All healing is simply the act of updating deeper structures which inform your being. Learning which occurred when the critical-analytical mind was weak is often automatic and charged with emotion.

Remember that the habits you are working on changing once served a useful purpose. It is important for you to acknowledge this if you are to learn to respect yourself and your life. To view outdated behavior patterns as "bad" will evoke guilt and create further useless bonds. No Blame. No Shame. Don't beat yourself up. If you are reading this, it is not too late to find peace and contentment.

As you begin to elicit new associations and construct new behavior, you will, from time to time, become aware of the less useful responses reappearing. This does not mean that you are going backwards. Rather, it signals that learning is taking place since, prior to learning, you would have not been conscious of outdated reactionary responses. When the old behavior appears, simply observe it and be respectful. Do not judge it. Just watch. In a moment or two it will recede into the background as it continues to undergo constructive reformulation.

As you gain more experience, your sense of power will increase.

The Multi-Layered Human Being

As you become aware of the styles in which you respond to your circumstances, you notice that your reactions are elicited from different layers of your being. Whatever you wish to change, you must engage at its level of communication.

No one operates from only one level of ego-functioning. Each ego state hears the same thing differently.

There are six primary levels of ego states.

The most primitive and survival-oriented level of ego operation is the *infant.* Learning that takes place at this level is primarily non-verbal in nature. We must access this level if we are to re-imprint the strong emotional-autonomic responses which are hard-wired into our neural systems.

The second level is the *child.* He is the explorer and creator. Learning takes place on verbal, imitative and non-verbal levels of communication. Though the child is more critical than the infant, strong emotional-automatic responses—which can act like hard-wiring—frequently occurs at this level.

The third level is the *parent.* The parent level is based on how the infant and the child relate to its caretakers. If the parent is critical, the child will learn guilt and shame. Creativity may be stifled at this point if the child learns that he is not good enough.

The fourth level is the *adolescent.* The adolescent is the precursor to the adult. He or she is trying out new behaviors and exploring sexual identity. The adolescent attempts to break away from the dependencies of childhood. This period is usually disturbing to everyone. Parents are required to shift roles and orientations. The pre-adult has adult desires with childhood dependencies. Co-dependency often arises when the adolescent is not able to find a sense of identity separate from the parent.

The fifth level is the *adult.*

The sixth level is the *Trans-personal* and deals with the Numinous.

Our subconscious often controls our reactions. If you really want to change, it is imperative to PAUSE, and learn to respond, rather than react. But first you must become aware of how your subconscious programs your reactions and enforces un-useful and painful behavior and perceptions of yourself and others.

Try This!
(Become a Deep Sea Diver)

If you want to dive into unknown neural seas, you will need something to write with and a calm mind. Put yourself in your Safe Place. If you have difficulty calming yourself down, try a glass of beer or wine, light a white candle, and play a recording of water sounds—rain, waterfalls, waves, etc.

The following exercise has been constructed to help you access the deeper regions of your mind through a process of Active Imagination, which is similar to a waking sleep state.

Under the Water Journey:
Part 1

IMAGINE, with your mind's eye, diving into a body of water. Put all your effort into your mental picture. Closing your eyes may help you have an enjoyable "hallucination." The scene you create becomes your own virtual reality.

The water you dive into may be the sea, a huge lake, an enormous pool or a river. Just make sure it's very deep. Take with faith the first image that comes. Let your imagination have its way and don't let your rational mind interfere in its fun.

Once you are submerged, pay attention to and take note of every detail you see, hear, touch, taste or smell. Be completely aware of what's going on around you as you swim or sink toward the bottom. Sense what's happening with your body. Is it cold, warm, shifting, thick, noisy, slimy, red, blue, dark, bright, sweet, salty? Take note of any things, alive or inanimate, which appear.

GO DEEP! As you reach the bottom, you will see something. This object appears only when you have reached the bottom. It is a spontaneous "vision"—a gift from your unconscious. Don't let your reason interfere with what you see, no matter how out of place, scary or silly it seems. Note what the object is. Appreciate it with your senses. Do you pick it up and carry it to the surface with you or do leave it undisturbed (perhaps for later collection)?

After imagining the scene, write it exactly as it happened. (You may want to imagine and write, imagine and write. This technique is somewhat like writing your dreams down when you are still half asleep. It takes some practice, but can be a great aid in your writing.) If you forget the details of your journey, simply close your eyes and imagine again. Note emotions and/or reactions to stimuli. Write as fast as you can—images, emotions and experiences of visualizations are forgotten quickly like dreams.

Do Not Worry About Grammar, Word Choice, Punctuation, or General Silliness.

Hallucinate and write for 25 minutes.

Part 2

AFTER RECORDING YOUR EXPERIENCE: Analyze the object found at the bottom of your "sea."

FREEWRITE (write without thinking) about what you think the *significance* of the object you found is. What does it *mean* to you? Does it symbolize anything? Can you connect the object in any way with anything that is currently going on in your life? Something in the past?

You might want to think about the following in relation to your object.

I secretly…
I feel…
I wish…
I must…

FREEWRITE about whether or not you took the object with you back to the surface, and why?

Repeat as necessary.

This Is Not A Test

Now you will begin to assess your strengths by becoming aware of your perceptual habits. Once you analyze and recognize the results, you begin to increase your flexibility.

For each of the following questions, give yourself a score of 1, 2, 3, 4 or 5. A score of 1 means very little. A score of 5 means a lot.

Question 1.
How much of the world do you perceive through thoughts and mental images?

Question 2.
How much of the world do you perceive through objects?

Question 3.
How much of a focused approach do you use in dealing with life?

Question 4.
How much discussion do you use in dealing with life?

Note: As you proceed you will become more aware that you use various methods in living life. No one uses one method exclusively.

Question 5.
How much do you use your visual sense to experience and understand reality?

Question 6.
How much do you use your auditory sense to experience and understand reality?

Question 7.
How much do you use your tactile sense to experience and understand reality?

Question 8.
How much do you use your olfactory sense to experience and understand reality?

Question 9.

How much do you process data linearly; that is, in a logical and sequential fashion?

Question 10.

How much do process data in a mosaic fashion?

Question 11.

How much do you expand and enhance your inputs and responses?

Question 12.

How much do you restrict and reduce your input and responses?

If you are waiting for an evaluation based on what your responses mean, you will not get it. Just review your responses and meditate on them. Think about whether you feel good about your style of living. Think about what you might want to change.

Finding Home in the State of Being

A Brief Autobiographical Note From An Author

My mother, upon noticing I would become restless and disillusioned with any course of study I pursued, finally asked me: "Just *what* are you searching for?" I considered myself a seeker, and acknowledged within my psyche an innate discontentment which I believed would be cured only when I found what I was looking for. After many years I decided I was looking for a place where I felt at home. Somewhere I could relax. Home was not to be found with my insane family. So where is my home?

I'd heard the expression, "Home is where the [metaphorical] heart is"—where one can love and be loved. But like the hearts of the 90% of the population who grew up in dysfunctional family situations, my heart was fickle, insecure and often hard to find due to its tendency to escape and hide frequently. I remembered something William Blake said in reference to home: "A bird, a nest; a spider, a web; man, friendship."

Yet, I had recently moved to Seattle, Washington and left all my friends in Los Angeles, California. I realized that it wasn't my friends I was escaping, but the image I had created of myself—an image I had provided to my friends, an image which my friends had learned to rely on. I moved to Seattle because I needed to break free of my past misery. I needed to rid myself of my false self, which was akin to a victim of unloving parents. I wanted to free myself from this image.

I also moved so I might be free to have what some might negatively refer to as a nervous breakdown, but what I now know was really a self-breakdown.

I moved away because I thought I could shed my false self without having to explain my change to my friends—who liked the image I wore.

In Seattle I found myself making new friends and subsequently found myself wanting to move again—to Prague this time. I had, to my chagrin, subconsciously built the same self-image for my new friends because I wanted their acceptance and love.

Again, I felt trapped by images which identified me as an offbeat sort: a writer; a painter; a quirky, optimistic and fiercely independent person on whom everyone could lean. Inside, I was scared and lonely. I felt like a loser and could not support myself financially.

I believed I was a fake and a phony and a failure. I wanted to find a place where I could let my guard down, be vulnerable, relax and share my insecurities. I wanted to let people care for me as I cared for them. I wanted a home where I would be free from my constant self-judgment, where I could just experience life and still feel worthwhile. Home, I decided, was a place where I wouldn't have to define myself as a "shoulder to cry on" or as an artist in order to be accepted. I could be me without limits.

Before escaping to Prague, I realized that I wasn't going to find a home by escaping again. What I needed to do was let go of my self-judgment and learn to accept myself—both as a success and a failure. I needed to let go of the drama of either/or and embrace both/and. I was neither fiercely independent nor pitifully dependent. The image which my friends knew me by *wasn't* altogether fake. I just showed them one side of myself.

My sense of humor didn't disappear, but the need to use humor as a mask to cover shameful emotions dissipated. I learned to express the other aspects of myself—my feelings of smallness, my fears, my sadness, my imperfections—and know that it was OK.

I learned that my tension and inability to relax was not simply caused by my failures to behave in a manner that my mother wanted me to. *Rather, the anxiety which provoked both isolation and the urge to flee was a result of* **repressing** *aspects of myself which I had learned were undesirable.* My mother was ashamed of weakness and I had learned to bottle up any emotions that revealed that I needed other people (interconnection) in order to be happy. I learned to be ashamed as well. And I was miserable trying to be the happy caretaker who never needed a shoulder to cry on or a partner to love.

I began to make a conscious effort to show those sides of myself which I felt would provoke rejection. At first my friends were taken aback. In fact, they chided me when I verbalized my feelings of weakness. They seemed to expect me to be constantly strong. I was the one who always had positive advice, the one who could pick them up when they'd fallen. They were frightened of this change in me. They'd learned to see me as a rock, a pillar of strength.

But now I was crumbling and that lent them a sense of instability.

Yet, a short time later, they accepted my change and began to give me the nurturing I needed at that time. How wonderful an experience it was to break down and cry in a friend's arms, to hear a friend say that everything will be all right, and to know that I was loved.

To me, this was a concept totally new—that I could be loved even with "imperfections." My friends even expressed that they enjoyed my company more now that I'd let down my guard and confessed my humanness. They felt freer to be themselves. I was finally on my way to finding what I was looking for. I am building my home.

Something to Consider

After almost forty years of experience as a student of human behavior, I discovered something which is very curious. What I have found is no secret, yet it seems so obvious that it is often ignored.

People who have a difficult time living contentedly seem to generalize and perceive *everything* as Either/Or. No matter what happens, every event or experience gets translated into a personal judgment of either "good" or "no good."

Many distressed people categorize themselves and others by these simple, yet un-useful definitions, and continually judge their experiences based on these categories.

1. I am fundamentally good.
2. I am fundamentally no good.

From these statements follow:

1. Others are fundamentally good.
2. Others are is fundamentally no good.

As you may notice, these thoughts and ideas are circular and self-perpetuating.

The crux of the problem is simple: If you assume that you are bad, everything you do is bad. If you assume you are good, everything you do is good. And the manner in which you perceive yourself and your actions will, subsequently, affect how you perceive your environment and circumstances. This "metaphysical generalizing" is very common, and can cause a lot of pain.

In contrast to such simplistic judgment, the happy Authentic Human *experiences* events and situations *without judgment*.

The authentic Self doesn't need to chronically judge himself, others, or his circumstances. He enjoys life's journeys, events and experiences. His sense of Self is non-comparative. Any comparisons he *may* make are not for the purpose of metaphysical self-evaluation, but simply to learn. Without the stress of judgment, this person can PLAY and live in the present.

Living in the now and without judgment is living authentically, uncritically and creatively. *Worth* is not relevant to living content-edly. The adult who perceives the world as an Authentic Self never thinks about self-worth. He accepts himself as simply BEING. Does a fetus consider whether it is worthy to be born?

If you find yourself constantly judging whether you are fundamentally good and worthy of life, you open yourself to a world of misery. Even if you decide that you are worthy, your judgment will be open to reinterpretation. These reinterpretations are usually provoked when some event happens that elicits a reaction that you have learned is bad.

Humans are the only living beings that question their worthi-ness to live. *Who or what event of the past taught you to question your right to live?* The Authentic or Natural Self is not in bondage to any fundamental metaphysical judgments.

Stop and Do It

Put yourself into your state of sanctuary and safety. Attempt to remember the circumstances which led you to question your worth. Write these down, but don't judge them.

Next, consider yourself in a state of crisis. Hold your breath. While in a state of crisis, imagine that your metaphysical self-judgments fade away. You are alive! There is no need to question your worthiness to take up space on earth. If you have a difficult time with this, imagine that you are a redwood tree. Trees cannot think, they simply grow.

Or watch your cat or dog. Do you think your cat questions whether she is worthy of life? Have you ever seen a suicidal dog?

You might begin to ask yourself whether you are fundamen-tally good or not because you're now conscious of the idea. If you are dwelling on such nonsense, don't be concerned. Your work here will bring you back to your Authentic Self.

HI! TENSION

While New Agers often preach that your thoughts and imagination *create* reality, it is more correct to say that your imagination *sustains* reality. What you mentally visualize enhances your emotional reactions and habitual behavior patterns.

Consider Crowley's parable concerning the basics of magick: One man on a train sees a second man carrying a cage and asks him what's in it.

"A mongoose," the second man answers, explaining that he's bringing it to his poor brother who suffers from *delirium tremens* and is bothered by snakes.

"But those are imaginary snakes," the first man says. "And this is an imaginary mongoose," the second man replies.

Imagination, when combined with focused will and an open mind, works miracles.

Imagination, when employed actively, is quite powerful. Yet both mental chatter and conscious imagination are forms of tension, even though the former often causes tension headaches, while the latter state is often desired. We make an *in-tension* to employ conscious imagination, while mental babbling is usually not something that we desire.

Many artists have confused creative energy and tension. They may complain that their lives lack peace and serenity, yet they purposely put themselves in crisis to elicit the tension which they believe supplies them with the creative energy necessary to create. There is a reason that so many artists commit suicide.

Yet tension and creative energy are usually perceived as opposite states. The best and most joyous art is born of calmness and peace, as it is easier to access creative energy when the mind is not exhausted by anxiety-producing mental chatter.

Recall the times you felt tense, but not energetic. Those who suffer from chronic stress often find themselves unable to get anything done. Now recall the times when you felt very energetic and calm. In which state did you feel more creative energy?

Don't believe that to feel energetic you must feel tense. Energy flows. Tension is *stuck energy*. Energy is creation and destruction. Tension is stagnation and restraint.

Inner peace is not the opposite of energy but rather the opposite of tension. Artistic inspiration flows when the mind is calm. Recall the times when you felt tired, but calm.

No one enjoys the feeling of tension in body-mind.

The feeling of tension is abhorred so much that political leaders have become experts in controlling the level of tension of the populous to fuel war, peace or economic spending. Events as tragic as war are deliberately used to evoke tension and create a common enemy and cries for retaliation, while declaring peace relieves tension—and gets the politician re-elected.

This is the same brainwashing technique which often results in the victim's placing her faith in the captor. Tension can be manipulated and utilized by politicians as a method of a negative reinforcement to control a population.

Most people will do just about anything to escape tension and anxiety. It is no surprise that tranquilizers and opiates are the most abused drugs in our society.

Tension is sometimes referred to as "body anxiety." We use terms such as "falling apart," "losing it" or "flipping out" to describe states of high anxiety. We know that anxiety is a direct cause of lowered immune response and dis-ease, yet doctors rarely treat the physical ailments caused by anxiety with a dose of stress-relieving Imagination or Visualization techniques.

Other terms sometimes associated with tension include:

— pressure
— strain
— stress
— uptight
— tautness
— disease
— panic
— uneasiness
— tight
— weak
— hypersensitive
— inert
— irritated

— colorless
— easily startled
— anxious
— pain
— nervous

Remember a time when you felt extraordinarily tense. Write your experience down in detail. As you write, note any changes in your body. Don't judge yourself. Just note your experience.

If you view tension as a balloon whose internal pressure is increasing, you are imagining the correct picture. The usual solution to this problem is adding substances into the balloon which reduce the tension.

For humans, these substances are often drugs, alcohol, exercise and talk therapy. If the tension continues to build, the balloon will burst and a nervous breakdown will occur.

Anyone who has used substances to reduce anxiety will tell you that it's a vicious cycle. Tranquilizers cause more anxiety in the long run in the same way that the chronic use of painkillers can lead to the experience of even more pain.

There are alternative methods, of course, such as employing the Imagination in Meditation.

The first goal of Meditation is reduce tension and to elicit abundant energy and serene calmness. The second goal is to provide the ground where the Numinous (the "Higher Self") can be "confronted." The third goal is the deliberate manipulation and conditioning of imagination to the "Will."

How Tense Are You?

Probably the most misunderstood relationship is that between the cognitive process and tension. While thinking can be enjoyable, if it is tension-based—such as worrying or obsessing about the future or the past—it can be uncomfortable. Compulsive thinking that is motivated by worry or tension can cause the body-mind to lose sleep, lower the immune system, and just make you miserable. But these "obvious" qualities of tension are really not so obvious at all.

Consider this analogy:

Let's say you have two ounces of milk in an eight ounce glass. If you add two more ounces of milk, the glass will not overflow. But if the glass already has seven ounces of milk in it, and you add the same two ounces, it *will* overflow.

If you are prevented from seeing the amount of milk already in the glass, you won't know how much you can add before the glass spills over.

Obviously, it is helpful to consciously assess what was already in the glass before you add more milk to it—at least if you want to keep from making a mess.

Tension that causes a mental or emotional overload is often due to the *tension baselines* of a person (the milk already in the glass) rather than with the current problem.

When we blame a certain circumstance for our "nervous break-downs" or "anxiety attacks," we are often missing the point. The immediate circumstance may be merely the "straw that broke the camel's back."

When we solve the immediate problem, we aren't addressing the real weight of our burdens. We continue to carry this tension unconsciously (living with our mind filled with milk, if you will) and wonder why we cannot handle the "normal" challenges which are natural to living.

Problem-solving (i.e., the resolution of the immediate issue associated to a present tension-causing experience) will not necessarily remove the discomfort a person feels if the baseline tension is high. It's more like pulling a weed, but leaving the root. When the glass is running over, you are unable to process common tensions of life. Then you become focused on the milk running over—which increases tension.

People ignore cognitive rational solutions to the specific issues because all they can think of is relieving the tension. The problem-solving aspect of the mind often shuts down. Thus, before the perceived problems can be solved, the base level of tension needs to be reduced.

High baseline tension is usually caused by the fact that your subconscious is holding on to past traumas and behaviors.

Once the base level of tension is reduced, the "straw that broke the camel's back" can be perceived as a straw, rather than as a catastrophe. In fact, once the baseline tension is at an appropriate level, problems that caused extreme anxiety may cease to seem like problems at all.

Your particular baseline level of tension is perceived as natural—for you. If your normal state is tense, you'll likely perceive this high baseline level as normal—as *self*—until a circumstance arises and you find yourself freaking out.

Of course, your perception of self may change when tension increases or decreases. Yes, sometimes a person will feel uncomfortable when tension is *decreased*. They have a sense of impending doom when they *relax*. This is because even a positive emotional charge can add to base levels of tension. The glass of milk doesn't care whether the added milk that causes it to overflow is fresh or sour.

When working on yourself, keep in mind that while specific issues feed emotional levels, your baseline tension levels determine your reactions to life's challenges. Your sense of identity is often tied to your baseline level of tension. In other words, you have become comfortable perceiving yourself and, consequently, reacting to the world around you as a very tense person.

After years of identifying with or being defined as a high strung, nervous person, the thought of being at peace might make you even more nervous.

If you find yourself resisting the image of yourself as a peaceful human being, it is due to the *fear of change*. The mere thought of changing your personality style often produces resistance which can sabotage positive change. Be wary and persevere!

Another Opportunity for Self-Interrogation

Ask yourself: Who Are YOU? Then ask yourself: Who taught you to be the YOU you've been for all these years. Then ponder this question: **Who do you want to be for the rest of your life?** TAKE PLENTY OF TIME AND WRITE THE ANSWERS IN YOUR JOURNAL.

How the Ego Works

A Metaphor

People are like balloons.

We are pumped up with air either by ourselves or others.

Therefore we deflate through our own and others' feelings and actions.

All of us need to be pumped up from time to time.

Most people are very porous and leak all the time. They need to be constantly pumped up. It's the world of a junky, always looking for a fix.

Others have leaks in specific areas and conceal their holes.

Tremendous energy and resources are used in pumping up or patching leaks.

Some seek adoration or worship—typical of narcissists or emotional vampires. These people need constant ego-pumping, but their gratification is short-lived. Once their "food" jumps through the hoop and proves their undying love, narcissistic types feel miserable again and up the ante. Sooner or later their "food" abandons them, they become deflated and search for another food source.

Many people hide or isolate themselves when they feel deflated, too ashamed to reach out for help. They don't admit that they feel deflated or bad about themselves, and often create personas or avatars. This can lead to disassociation. This type of person is becoming increasingly common. Some even think that having a social network of friends that they've never met is normal social activity. This is a very lonely way to live.

Others seek social inferiors who will look up to them, even if their own esteem is a figment of their imagination. (As Dirty Harry put it, "You are a legend in your own mind.") If you constantly act as if you are superior to others, even though inside you feel worthless, you might be labeled an egomaniac, or even a sociopath.

Don't feel guilt or shame if you've done this. Laugh at yourself. Sometimes it can be really funny to watch ourselves manipulating, imagining or begging for an ego fix.

When people feel deflated they usually feel hopeless and angry at life. Some even blame "God" for their problems.

Many people also suffer from the simultaneous desire for applause and intense stage fright. They crave approval, yet are horrified of humiliation. The fear causes deflation of the ego, followed by self-hatred—particularly if they do not face their fear. Everything seems catastrophic to these people.

An ego-centered person will seek situations where they can safely pump up their ego. They are very cautions about entering situations which might deflate them. The concept of practicing true humility can be immensely helpful to people who tend to puff their egos up to the point of over-inflation.

When one over-inflates the ego (or false self), the elation is often followed by depression. Imagine a balloon pumped up with too much air: it pops and the pieces are scattered. The ego can be helpful at times, but it is also insubstantial. To use the balloon analogy: the ego is sometimes just a lot of hot air. If you analyze the people in your life, you might find that there are more ego-centric people than you imagined.

When a person pumps himself up *in a socially approved manner,* he is labeled "normal." Put a picture of your family on your desk. Buy a few certificates of achievement at the stationary store. Suggest an idea that pumps up everyone's ego. Can you hear the applause?

When the leaks are severe and a person uses *anti-social* means to pump himself up, he might come to think of himself as a demigod. Others might call him a psychopath. Hitler is a prime example of this type.

Porous or thin-skinned, sensitive people are easily deflated. Some throws tantrums. Others become martyrs who compulsively sacrifice themselves and pump their ego-balloons by thinking they are self-sacrificing. These people are professional victims.

Then, there is the chronically depressed person. This type finds it impossible to pump up his imaginary ego-balloons. He may try psychiatrists, drugs, etc., but it is all to no avail because, in his heart, he realizes it is a trick.

There is also the perpetual seeker. Spiritual seekers find teachers, saints or powerful groups to identify with. By doing this they pump themselves up. Alas, the moment their idol errs or displays a character defect, these folk realize that their idol has clay feet. Usually they feel temporarily elated since they now feel that they are superior to their former idol. After a period of deflation and elation, they frequently find another idol who will eventually disappoint them and the cycle is repeated.

Most addicts fall into the seeker category. They relieve the pain of their leaking balloon and, at the same time, blow themselves up out of all proportion. Some just relieve the pain and go over their list of humiliations and defeats. Whatever their *real* accomplishments, they diminish to themselves and exaggerate to others.

The drunk is a prime example. He inflates himself and then suffers deflation. He talks at others even though they show annoyance. When drunk he is full of pride and an overbearing appearance. When sober he feels small and totally deflated, his body is weak, and his shame is great.

A person with a leaky ego-balloon frequently compares himself to others. She imagines faults in others to pump herself up. Some act out in ways that deflates the other. This is typical in domestic abuse, where one partner blames any insecurity or ego-deflation on his or her partner.

A leaky person is self-conscious, often obsessing over an imagined or real insult. He wastes his energy on rationalizing who is at fault, usually alternating from blaming himself to blaming the other. In the end, he only proves that his ego is a leaky balloon.

Regardless of the type, a person with a leaky ego-balloon is in a lot of pain. A few people, however, are less porous and do not need to be pumped up by themselves or others. These people have *character*.

What causes a leaky ego-balloon? Usually the person was overindulged in some aspects of life, while deeply rejected in others. For example, imagine a mother who put on rubber gloves and cursed every time she had to change her daughter's diapers. The child never learned that she was okay and married an abusive partner. Divorced and living with her abusive mother, she is still convinced that she needs to be no less than perfect if she is to be loved.

Intimate relationships are excellent devices for mutual pumping and leak stoppage; however, many relationships have a dual purpose and also function as the means to deflate the other and the self. The angry husband inflates himself by constantly picking on his martyred wife. At a moment of crisis, guilt strikes and his ego deflates. Now it is her turn to inflate her ego by telling him how he couldn't live without her support—until she goes too far and feels guilty.

To rid oneself of the guilt or the feeling of being unloved, one blames the other for their feelings. In fact, both partners need so much unconditional love that they have no true love to give one another. They are both in too much pain.

They do not ever STOP and realize that it is their EGO that is leaking and the only way to repair the leak is from the inside out. This requires direct participation and work.

To repair the situation each person has to climb inside their balloon and honestly look around. This is a hard job as the entrance is tight and twisted. It's like the birth canal, except in reverse. Fortunately, it CAN be DONE…

The first step is to accept that you have a leaky ego-balloon and become completely accountable for what you have done—and continue to do—to inflate your ego. Often, you need to take a leap of faith since the tricky ego can easily find *real* causes to blame. No one has a perfect life. Taking responsibility is the first step of the inward journey to becoming a self-change artist. It is also the first step toward responding to life with clarity.

This is important. You can only begin the process of becoming the artist of your own life if you accept full and complete responsibility, acknowledge your feelings honestly and sincerely, and LET GO OF GUILT AND SHAME.

This step builds character. If you continue to feel guilt and shame, you have not accepted responsibility for your condition. You have, in essence, not accepted *life*.

Don't dread this step. Once you accept who you are, the forces sealed in the heart begin to pour out. Not only will you begin to love your Self, your love will begin purifying the world.

FIGHT, FLIGHT, OR BE STILL

The autonomic nervous system (ANS) is commonly known as the flight-or-fight bio-survival system. It is designed to help organisms respond rapidly to life threatening situations. You know the feeling: your heart-rate increases, you're temporarily capable of lifting heavy objects, running like a gazelle, and even leaping across buildings in a single bound. The ANS is primarily a non-cognitive system. *Thus simple cognitive intervention has a minimal effect.* (So much for positive thinking?)

Those who panic at the drop of a hat are prone to inherently high tension levels. When there are high levels of tension, the ability to reduce a specific stressor is difficult, making many who suffer from chronic tension poor candidates for normal types of verbal intervention.

Anything—and we mean *anything*—which adds to their already high level of "readiness" is experienced as "dangerous" and causes an anxiety reaction. These people may be called chronic or life-style "phobics." It is important to keep in mind that it is not the object or situation which upsets them, but their *readiness to be tense.* Unfortunately, when a situation triggers a high-stress attack in these people, innocent bystanders suffer. Those who suffer from chronically high tension often beat their children, spouses and themselves.

For some people, common methods to counter tension simply do not work. Vacations seem to add more stress to their lives, counting to ten is impossible, and telling themselves to relax is futile. Because of the high levels of arousal, tension itself is something to fear; the onset of tension simply breeds more tension. It is similar to the case of the insomniac who fears his inability to sleep so intensely that it is the fear of not sleeping itself which is causing the insomnia. This fear of fear, if you will, creates a vicious circle which is frequently difficult to extinguish without the use of drugs or alcohol.

When the autonomic nervous system is inappropriately "taught" to respond to certain situations, trigger words, or symbols, it can become hyper-active. Further, if the autonomic system has been inappropriately forced to remain active for a long period of time before resolution is allowed, it becomes dulled. For example, a child who must wait three hours for his father to come home to punish him may develop a chronic state of flight/fight reactivity. Because the ANS remains active for a longer time than natural conditions would allow, muscular tension, increased heart rate, and general anxiety become confused with the natural state of being. The state of tension becomes habitual simply because a person gets used to it. Moreover, because children usually can neither run nor fight, they may develop an overactive anticipatory fantasy life.

The net result is that the ANS becomes adept at reacting to a set of internal cues and images which often have little to do with the situation at hand. The person reacts habitually, rather than responding in the present. In other words, the person does not live life in the here-and-now, but rather is in bondage to strong emotional reactions caused by former experiences which have now become internally programmed. This is the cause of the biochemical-neural bonds which were discussed in the chapter *Breaking the Bonds of Fear.*

When this type of learned reaction is coupled with the child's own fantasies or "taboo" desires, the entire autonomic system begins to feed on itself. The child feels intense anxiety over its own thoughts and feelings. When the child becomes an adult, "little" things can become gigantic issues, and a real crisis can become a catastrophe.

The person is enslaved by an over-reactive nervous system (his own reactions) and is not responding to circumstances of present existence. In fact, when enslaved by an over-reactive nervous system, even the act of assessing one's personal reality can become a difficult job.

The interaction of an over-active fantasy life, repressed fears and desires, and an over-reactive nervous system makes a debilitating combination.

Being Here Now Is Easier Said Than Done

Mystics, Sages and Wise men and women throughout the ages have consistently suggested that living in the present is a key to bliss—if not heaven itself. In Aldous Huxley's utopian novel *Island*, parrots were trained to say, "Here and Now Boys" in an effort to remind the islanders to keep their thoughts on the present. Ram Dass' text *Be Here Now* has become a classic. And living in the present is, of course, the basic goal of Zen, Yoga and many forms of Mysticism.

While living in the *now* has, ironically, never been an effortless goal, modern society seems particularly adverse to nurturing such a way of life. And for those living with a chronically high tension baseline, the ability to live in the present, free from the bonds of past or future, seems virtually impossible.

When the ANS baseline is high, thoughts about the future easily create "future physiologic" reactions in the present. The person has fight-or-flight reactions to phantoms. Thoughts about the past create a "past physiologic" reaction. As Karl Pribram noted, our actions are "controlled" by both a "feed-forward" and a "feed-back" system.

The here-and-now is continually blurred by these "physiologic" prejudices, making the individual respond more to these "generated physiologic reactions" than those elicited by present circumstances. It becomes difficult for individuals to "give" themselves to the moment and thus experience the moment to the fullest. Their internal state consists primarily of interactive physiologic reactions to the past and anticipation of the future. For these people, the future—as well as the past—discolors the *now*. The present, in all its richness, becomes blurred, confounded and confused.

ANS: The Bottom Line When It Comes to a Happy Mind

Every child is born with an autonomic nervous system (ANS) which has a particular hard-wired genetic baseline. Due to genetics, some children respond more heavily to emotions or physical discomfort than others. For example, some cry when slightly hungry, others don't.

Except in rare cases, most children's inborn ANS baseline falls within a healthy and functional range. This baseline can be affected by the circumstances in which a child develops. In other words, since children can't win arguments with adults, nor escape without adult assistance (i.e., they are dependent on adults), an environment which continually threatens them will lead to either a very high or very low ANS baseline.

Depending on the type and the duration of the threatening conditions which a child must endure, the ANS baseline can be distorted to such an extent that the child begins to live in a state of chronic preparation or chronic deadness. After a period of time, this state of chronic guardedness slips into the unconscious and the person regards it as normal and natural.

The baseline ANS can be elevated at any particular period within the child's developmental process. If the circumstances responsible for the elevation occur for a long period of time and over many developmental stages, numerous external and internal cues will be conditioned to this level of arousal.

The baseline ANS may also be elevated during a period of trauma. This is the case with many adults who have "forgotten" a traumatic experience, but continue to react in negative ways to certain triggers.

A person can spend a lifetime in therapy with little fundamental change to a high Baseline ANS (BANS).

Not only do parents affect a child's BANS, every culture *desires* a particular BANS. For example, people raised in Western cultures usually have a higher baseline (more stress) than those raised in a traditional Polynesian culture.

As a group, Americans have a high baseline. Violence, suicide and child abuse are rampant in the U.S., as are depression, addiction and compulsions. Many people exist by popping a chemical cocktail every day.

Even people who seem successful find themselves constantly on the verge of a nervous breakdown because of their high baseline ANS. One has only to attend an Alcoholics Anonymous meeting in Beverly Hills and listen to a celebrity speak to know how common this is.

Doctors, lawyers and CEOs were often raised in environments which promoted a high baseline ANS, and learned to equate pushing themselves as hard as they can as a way to keep control and feel loved. Their BANS is so high that they are prone to various forms of destructive self-medication.

It is our view that most forms of self-destructive behavior are primarily attempts to reduce the painful feelings associated with a high BANS. Rage, drugs, alcohol, over-eating, deviant sexual behavior, etc. are all attempts to turn down the volume of a hyperactive neural system.

HAR AND THE CREATION OF THE FALSE SELF

High Autonomic Reactivity (HAR) refers to the increased probability of a non-cognitive reaction to internal and/or external factors. In other words, a person *reacts* to a given stimulus according to a subconscious program, rather than *responding* to the actual situation.

The reactionary behavior produced by HAR has no survival value—it frequently sabotages a person's goals—even though psycho-physiologically the organism reacts "as if" its survival depends on such habitual reactions.

HAR acts as an over-readiness to react. The process is self-perpetuating. People suffering from HAR have been described as ultra-sensitive, anxious, emotionally flat, depressed, socially incompetent, hostile, unmotivated, fearful, shy or manipulative. They are usually so wrapped up in their own feelings that they are unable to respond authentically to a present situation.

HAR makes it difficult for such people to see things for what they are. Everything is highly charged with potential dangers and rewards. Yet, since the origin of HAR is primal, most experiences feel disappointing. Nothing is ever enough, nothing truly satisfies, because the ability to respond naturally to any given circumstance—what we call "response-ability"—is blocked.

The person suffering from HAR resides in a state of chronic stress which renders him incapable of living life in the present.

He has unconsciously built a suit of psycho-physical armor which life cannot penetrate. The person is no longer open to life, but resides in a state of rigid contraction: Self is surrounded by self and life (LOVE) is locked out. He has built a shell that limits himself to a myopic lifestyle where natural human joy is rarely, if ever, experienced. This is the nightmare of the walking dead. And, believe it or not, in our society it is very common.

Often alcohol, drugs, sex, shopping sprees, and other such "addictions" provide *some* relief from the pain, but these forms of self-medication do not permanently relieve the pain of being chronically on guard. Nor do they crack the shell which separates Self from Life.

Many who suffer from HAR attempt to alleviate their pain by mental processes—logic, reason or brutal self-analysis—with little permanent change. The level of tension is so ingrained in the psycho-physical body that trying to talk oneself out of the state of chronic tension often leads to more tension. Self-medicating— whether drugs, food, alcohol or sex—often leads to higher levels of HAR as these actions often cause more shame to an individual who already lacks confidence.

Yet, individuals who suffer from HAR are increasing. More and more people classify themselves as alcoholics, drug addicts, over-eaters, anorexics, over- and under-achievers, co-dependents, video-game addicts, etc. Many seek relief through 12-step programs. There are now 12-step programs for virtually every dis-ease of anxiety. There is even a 12-step program for artists who cannot control their muse. Most individuals involved in 12-step programs suffer from HAR and are looking for relief from chronic tension. They feel relieved that they are not alone in their suffering. Since 12-step programs harbor tenets such as "Power-lessness" and "Let go and Let God", they attempt to cease to blame themselves. However, as any old-timer in a Program will attest, the success rate is low, particularly when it comes to alcoholism and drug abuse. Many people in A.A. and N.A. do end up either dead, in jail or insane.

HAR frequently leads to actual physical distress and the body will develop automatic defenses or more armor. The body literally tenses up to the point of chronic muscle tension. Many sexual dysfunctions stem from HAR.

Some people who suffer from chronic tension aren't even aware of it. They experience HAR reactions as necessary, rather than learned and circumstantial. Defense structures fall into two very broad categories known as "funneled-confined" and "barreled-reactive."

Broadly speaking, the *funneled-confined* type tends to restrict *input*. This type of person will tune out life and refuse to let anyone know his real self. He is often labeled as having a fear of intimacy or as being excruciatingly shy. Oftentimes the funnel-confined person, while outwardly seeming OK, will suffer greatly within and will punish herself by binging and purging, drinking secretly, or any of many compulsive habits that will leave her wallowing in shame.

The *barreled-reactive* type has difficulty in restricting *output*. He will usually find himself in one relationship after another. He is often the life of the party, but suffers from emptiness or loneliness.

The automatic, habitual quality of HAR makes the sufferer believe that her HAR, as well as her coping mechanisms, are her true self. She perceives herself as sick. This is not true. The tension and addictions produced by HAR is a false self. She has literally become her own shadow. As John Bradshaw noted, "Once one becomes a false self, one ceases to exist psychologically." The person has lost the human capacity to respond naturally. Alice Miller calls the creation of the false self "soul murder." And while a person who has created a false self often suffers—usually from an intense feeling that something essential is lacking in her self— therapy usually doesn't work.

The armor that separates self from life keeps the sufferer from experiencing the fluidity of life, both its ecstatic joys and sorrows. Authentic emotions are fluid.

Therapy is often ineffective as many therapists unknowingly treat the false self, hoping to convert it into a functional part of society. Or they label the person as resistant to change, when the patient is really resistant to losing his false sense of himself.

When Habitual Fear Paves the Road to Failure

Extreme levels of *High Autonomic Reactivity* (HAR) create an internal environment where molehills become mountains.

Minor and non-threatening situations are often built up into a catastrophe simply because of the high level of HAR. Most therapists find it difficult to help those who suffer from this, particularly if the therapist pays too much attention to the details of the environmental stimuli and the patient's explanations. Since the patient's "reality" is often exaggerated by her internal anxiety, the therapist is treating a false reality.

Treating specific symptoms, complexes and situations is useless until the general level of HAR is reduced—although, in practice, "life incompetencies" as well as HAR, are often treated at the same time.

The therapist often has trouble getting the patient to cooperate, since significant baseline changes in the level of HAR create a "rejection phenomenon" similar to organ rejection. Many sufferers of HAR can't give up their chronically tense state of being. They are used to being in pain and fear, and can't even fathom being different. Some may identify with martyrs or saints in order to defend their false self. The fear of breaking up with the false self can be overwhelming.

HAR is most often expressed during social interactions. Thus HAR damages one's relationships, even though the sufferer rarely realizes how he lost his wife or job, as his reactions have been so internalized.

While HAR levels can be decreased to some degree by learning new behavior patterns (e.g., from bio-feedback techniques), the general state of the person cannot be *significantly* altered this way.

This makes re-conditioning of habits and self-defeating attitudes difficult at best, since the level of the flight-or-fight response is continuously high. Such people are stuck in a world of reaction. They react according to a pre-programmed set of triggers and fantasies that have little to do with the present situation. *They are literally enslaved by the past.* Even a good therapist will have a difficult time unraveling the false self and getting through to the authentic self.

People of average (i.e., normal) HAR should be considered unhealthy since the population itself is pathological. This is one reason why even "happy" events, such as weddings and parties, lead to increased HAR, as well as the need to reduce it with drugs, alcohol or arguments. We have all heard the saying that "Life was just going too well…"

So…what can sufferers of HAR do? If you've done the exercises so far, you're on your way. KEEP ON READING! KEEPING ON WORKING!

PART III

THE ENDLESS MEDITATION

Or: How To Undo It Yourself and Save Time and Money

Some Issues Concerning Meditation

While the stress relief and awareness that meditating causes is desirable, achieving it is easier said than done. Ask anyone who practices Zazen, Pranayama or Centering Prayer. Quieting the chatter of the mind takes work! One reason that Westerners have difficulty is that we live a more complex life style than in the Eastern world.

In addition, our approach to life is more active and we are more preoccupied with our individual aspirations, where the Eastern world is more communal.

Westerners invest more energy creating a sense of self, or an ego, even though this self is often false.

Joseph Campbell once mentioned that Westerners find Eastern techniques of meditation difficult due to the fact that Western culture actually causes an individual to develop a harder ego. He likened a Western Ego to an eggshell which would not crack with a simple tap of Yogic energy.

The Western Method of "Mental Health"

Psychology vs. Thymotology

In the West when we are emotionally troubled, we seek the advice of physicians or psychotherapists and are labeled "ill."

However, it is not *we* who are ill most of the time; rather, it is our lifestyles and value systems. Our style of functioning severely interferes with a healthy life.

The human species is not inherently pathological and the individual is not born "sick." Except in rare cases of brain or organ damage, the concept of pathology doesn't apply. These ideas are not yet very popular in psychiatric circles and are more in accord with rebels such as psychiatrist Thomas Szasz, M.D. (whose views are expressed in his book *The Myth of Mental Illness*), and the famed Robert Lindner, Ph.D.

Most of modern day clinical psychology is utter nonsense and myth. And while this might come as a shock to those who want to believe that science has the absolute cure, many rebel-minded researchers have recently spoken out against the reliability and validity of the most popular forms of psychological theory and practice. Following the lead of quantum physics, the so-called science of psychology is beginning to realize that we can only know what we can know. No theory, no matter how good it sounds, can take the place of facts.

Mistaking the Psyche With Another Ology

The word "psychology" has an interesting history. The early Greeks had a two-phase theory of the soul. One aspect was called *thymos* which was concerned with emotion and thought.

For the early Greeks the lungs and the diaphragm were the seat of *thymos*. They thought this because breath (*pneuma*) and words contained air, the "element" associated with thought. When people spoke, the chest and the diaphragm moved...

The other aspect was called *psyche,* the origin of the word psychology. According to Homer, the psyche was immortal, yet contained no memory of prior lives.

Most Greek philosophers posited that the immortal *psyche* had minimal involvement with earthly existence, and rarely interfered with day-to-day consciousness (except in cases of prophecy, wherein *thymos* and psyche married).

(As time progressed, the Greek philosophers unified *thymos* and *psyche* and relocated the soul to the brain. Some Greeks theorized that information entered the soul through the breath or *pneuma.* The phrase "breath of life" came about due to the belief that spirit entered the body via breath, as well as departed the body when breathing ceased.)

Ironically, the etymological definition of the word "psychology" concerns the study—or "ology"—of one's immortal soul. (What is now considered Eschatology.) Pathological psychology refers to the study of the sick immortal soul.

According to the original Greek definitions, modern psychology would be better defined as thymotology, which is the study of emotion and thought, and clinical psychology would be clinical thymotology, or the study of sick emotion and thought.

Today, any learned person who understands the scientific method would consider absurd the numerous and untestable theories posited by clinical psychologists. In fact, many of their theories sound similar to those of the early Greeks which were often based on metaphor and simplex observations. However, the Greeks may be excused for their fallibilities since they were not privy to the knowledge we have today of physiology, chemistry, biology and experimental psychology.

Yes, The Dice Are Usually Loaded

One quality of a real science is predictability, but modern clinical psychology only "predicts" what has already happened. This, of course, is not prediction at all but just simple labeling, and is akin to a gambler who shouts "7" after the dice land and show numbers 3 and 4. Further, many psychologists often misdiagnose the events they do see (i.e., misread the dice), causing further confusion in the soul of an already confused patient.

[I would venture that in a thousand years anthropologists will be unable to perceive a structural difference between what we today call "clinical psychology" and "theology." Both "ologies" attempt to take on the mantle of science to give themselves a sense of "respectability" (e.g., theologians have constructed the word "creationism" to "compete" with the word "Darwinism" and provide a veneer of hard science, but without any understanding of the *substance* of science). Both "ologies" seek to explain events *after* they occur and, when challenged, quickly abandon science and appeal to faith.]

While every clinician claims that his particular methods help his patients, there are few clear-cut studies that demonstrate the usefulness of one type of treatment over another. What seems to help is an empathetic ear and time. But most of us aren't willing to spend seven to ten years suffering through the healing process. Nor should a patient pay off a clinician's mortgage because that clinician is adept at using circular logic, fuzzy concepts, and pseudo-explanations to keep his hopeful patient in therapy for years. A person can be her own best psychologist **if she *works* at it...and for a fraction of the cost of hiring a "professional."**

Many of the practices of clinical psychology are so convoluted that they include numerous escape clauses. When the patient doesn't agree with the diagnosis of the psychologist, follow his directions, or get better, many "therapists" blame the patient, and accuse him of being in denial or resisting "treatment."

If a therapist is accused of being non-scientific, he will often retort that therapy is more art than science. However, I think that there is little about psychotherapy that is artistic...

The Tower of Psycho-Babble:
Speaking in Psycho-Tongues, or the Rationalization of God

Today's psychological theories are reminiscent of various theologies, but without the "benefit" of a god.

Psychiatrists and psychologists often adhere to the theology of the atheist. (This might seem to be an oxymoron, but it is quite a common state of being. Theological atheism does *not* profess faith in a god, but rather requires faith in a *god-substitute*, usually an appeal to an "authority" combined with an avid adherence to the dogma of a particular school of thought.)

A theology consists of a set of dogmas, creeds and doctrines fueled by needs and belief. If one accepts the assertions of a theological school to be the One and Only Truth, and if proper logic is used, its conclusions will inevitably seem true. Of course, none of the numerous contradictory assertions can ever be tested since these "truths" reside in the realm of metaphysics.

> **"What the Thinker thinks, the Prover proves."**

Choosing a Therapy Is a Game of Craps

I [C.S. Hyatt] have known hundreds of clinicians; in fact, I used to be one. I have observed that regardless of clinical theory or approach, one-third of all patients get better, one-third get worse, and one-third remain the same. Moreover, I have observed that often the client himself provided the cure.

The people who earn the reputation of being the best "healers" are usually those who help the client help herself. When healing occurs, it is not scientific in terms of theory or method, but rests on the relationship between therapist and client—or a roll of the dice.

I remember being referred to a psychotherapist when I was an undergraduate student. I was going through a divorce and needed some counseling. It was the sixties and I was a hippie. When I walked into his office both of us shuddered. He was wearing a suit and had a crewcut, while I wore weird clothes and had long hair and a beard. Needless to say our encounter didn't last past the first session. He couldn't understand me and I couldn't understand him. We didn't speak the same language and we certainly didn't inhabit the same world. I went back to the University's referral office, complaining. The secretary found a fellow more suited to me, both literally and figuratively.

A Theory By Any Other Name...

Contemporary psychotherapy has taken a systems approach to treatment. Like Freud, who appropriated the methods of theology and hydraulics to build his theories, system theorists borrow their structure from information and game theory to achieve the goal of normalcy. Many believe that such a foundation provides authority and scientific status to psychological practices since the structure is based on a scientific model. However, borrowing "scientific" concepts and applying them randomly in a different context (such as the mind) does not give psychotherapy scientific validity.

In conclusion, the success rate of clinical psychology is mostly based on faith, personality, empathy and time. This is not to argue that people aren't helped by these factors, but so what? It does make one wonder if and how psychotherapy has progressed since Freud's time.

What is called clinical psychological theory consists of assertions which, like theology, are as impossible to disprove as they are to prove.

But for something to be included in the realm of science, *by definition* its assertions must be *testable* (i.e., capable of being shown to be false). If it is not in the realm of science, it doesn't deserve the status of science.

We do not claim that our methods are "scientific," although some have been tested scientifically and have proven effective. All we claim is that our experience and the experience of others demonstrate their utility in helping you gain the goals of high energy and serenity.

MENTAL HEALTH MEANS FUNCTIONING LIKE AN AVERAGE PERSON

If you are an exceptional person—and this doesn't simply mean creative, but someone who is different from the societal conception of the normal (i.e., *average*) person—you'd best avoid psychotherapy. Unless you find an exceptional therapist.

If you find yourself feeling insecure or worthless because you can't function as a cog in the mechanical wheel of modern society, you may feel the need to seek help so you can conform, be understood and understand. It is often lonely being odd.

You need only turn on the evening news to realize that the machine of present day society does not provide a "happy" life. Every societal system was created by those in power to benefit what they value. William Blake wrote, "I must create my own System or be enslav'd by Another's."

Clinical psychology and psychotherapy are based on the theology of the State, and the theology of any culture is entwined with the theology of its founders. For example, when the Emperor Constantine was a Pagan, his empire was Pagan. When, near the end of his life, he converted to Christianity, the foundation for a New Empire was formed.

In any society a psychologically "healthy" person lives more or less in accordance with the tribal habits and mores of that society. In the West, that means a "healthy" person resembles an anemic follower of Jehovah and Jesus Christ.

A psychologically healthy person embodies the prayer of the un*response*-able: "Not My Will, but Thine." He doesn't cause trouble and obeys the law of the powerful. He who breaks the rules gets kicked out of the Garden of Innocence and into the harsh, but *living,* World of Experience.

If you consider yourself a rebel in any sense of the word, it might behoove you to stay away from psychotherapy—unless, of course, your therapist is also a rebel. Beware: It is unlikely that your therapist practices the art of conscious rebellion, or will respond to you as an individual and provide *useful* remedies. In psychotherapeutic circles, condoning useful practices often requires doing something that might be characterized as "unethical." Most psychologists will not risk their hard-earned license...

Dr. Hyatt's Story:
Why I Quit the Business of Psychotherapy

I quit because the time came that I could no longer help a patient without incurring personal risk. At one time if a person came to me for help because he was (say) highly introverted and wanted to learn to be more extroverted, I would take him out on the town and observe how he behaved. I would then take him back to the office and help teach him the necessary skills. I would then take him out on the town once again and guide him through his new behaviors. I would sit in a bar and drink with him. I might even invite women over to our table for conversation.

However, effective as such techniques might be, to a licensing board this behavior would be considered highly unethical. In their terms, I have established a "dual relationship" with my client. I have shared drinks and food with him. I may have visited him at his home to see how he lives. I may even have gone to parties with him. After he leaves me as a therapist I might enjoy having a drink with him from time to time, or we may even share a common interest like horse racing and go to the track together. Yet for this type of treatment—which could properly be labeled scientific field study—I could lose my license. So instead I was faced with having to practice in a way which was less effective, more costly and less enjoyable to my clients...but safer to myself.

I once treated a severe drinker (alcoholic). He had been isolating himself and drinking in secret, and was up to a liter or more a day. I showed him how to control his drinking by simply getting together with him and sharing drinks with him. He reduced his drinking to two or three drinks a day and a two-day binge once a month.

But before I proceeded along these lines I suggested Alcoholic Anonymous—not because I thought it was best for him, but because it was regarded as the "accepted" treatment. A.A. failed to help him so I tried this alternative method.

I did this in the 1970s, long before the current addiction craze. Of course, today a licensing board would consider my methods highly unprofessional. And yet, many years later my client is still living his life happily as a "moderate" drinker.

Regardless of my client's success, most psychologists today would not attempt to help someone with such an alternative treatment (i.e., showing an alcoholic how to drink moderately and without the shame and guilt which causes most alcoholics to binge). As agents licensed by the State, psychologists who try such "non-professional" (read: "not entrenched in academic theory") would be in danger of losing their license to practice.

A psychotherapist's license is his livelihood. His position in society is based on his ability to use his license to earn an income. As most people who have gone to therapy can attest, the typical orientation toward safe, lengthy and ineffective treatment benefits the therapist economically since his clients remain painfully sick, and continue to pay for years. It's hard to start over with a new therapist once you "invest" in one.

Often the therapist cannot comprehend the world of the client. If the therapist is not allowed to put himself into that world, how will she help him?

Many psychotherapists come from a background completely alien from that of his patient. What does a middle class housewife with a degree know about a prostitute or a homosexual? Only what she has been told. Sadly, housewives and divorcees make up the majority of psychotherapists. They want to feel better about themselves, and so they get a career that will make them respected while allowing them more freedom than a nine to five job.

Dr. Hyatt's "Therapy Revisited"

I left my practice in 1979. In the late 1980's I decided to investigate the therapy game again. I interviewed for a number of jobs, did a lot of observing, and gave considerable thought to opening a private practice again. I was offered a few positions, but declined them all. I was turned off by the rigidity, the insurance forms, the rules, the lies, and the fear of not being able to be myself and do things my way. I hate doing things "by the book," and it was apparent to those who interviewed me that I didn't fit the description of a "team player." So I gave up the idea and focused on my own methods. This book is one result.

THE EGO AND THE ART OF STAYING LIQUID

Different people mean different things when using the word "Ego". Here are but a few connotations of YOUR EGO:

— Soul
— Self
— Subconscious
— Higher consciousness
— Spirit
— Mind
— Sublime self
— Inner man
— Psyche
— Individuality
— Personality
— Character
— Esteem

If you agree with the popular idea that you possess an ego, it will be time well spent to contemplate what you really mean—and what others might mean—when throwing that word around.

A popular definition is that the ego is simply the *self* or *personality*. But which aspect of self or personality? The concept of a person with a "big ego" differs from the concept of a person with "high self esteem." The latter seems a more attractive fellow than the former. However, this is ludicrous since the degree to which one "esteems" oneself is necessarily tied up with the ego.

Also, if we define the ego as the self or personality, we automatically indicate a dualism in our natures. The ego becomes relational to something *beyond* the self or personality, a super-ego or a higher self or an authentic self.

If the ego is defined as an aspect of our being, ask yourself: Who wrote the definition?

Stop And Consider This Question

What exactly are you referring to when you say "my ego"? Who or what decides what your ego is? Who or what defines what your ego is? Does your ego reside with another "being" in your head? Are you the proud parent of one, two, three or more brains?

If You See Your Ego On the Road, Kill It!

For the sake of further discussion, let's agree with the popular consensus that the ego is our self-concept—that is, the way in which we define our self based on our experiences. In this sense, the ego is a complex matrix of definitions and images *created by others and your self in relation to how you react to others and how they react to you.* If this is true, your ego is the sum of your memories, both referential and emotional, which you processed from the sounds, touch, sights, tastes and smells which you have experienced throughout your life.

The analogy of alchemy is appropriate here in that your ego is a substance created from the processing of various elements of life experience that were combined within the alembic of your being.

In this context, the ego is a conclusion. Now this is important, as the definition of *the ego is created by how people react to you, and vice-versa, from the moment you are born until the moment you die.*

Of course, the ego is more easily fixed in the early years and hence is less likely to change significantly as you get older. It is as if, at a certain point in time—usually at the endpoint of what psychologists call the formative years—the ego calcifies or hardens. No longer plastic, it becomes a shell—or a tomb.

Your present self-concept is based on *how others have reacted to and defined you **prior to your ability to defend your true self, rationalize, argue, beg or become the artist of your own being and life.*** *You were created by circumstances rather than choice. More of a prison than a choice.*

To rid your self of this *forced* ego is a great joy, whether your fundamental definition of yourself is positive or negative. This is a **learned** personality, not your character. It is the ego or false self which mystics of all cultures suggest you KILL. Go ahead, Make Your Day! Don your best Dirty Harry impersonation and **Shoot Your False Ego Dead.**

BUT WAIT! Don't finger that trigger yet. Before you *kill this ego,* you must first don the hat of Socrates and get to *know* this self. You and your ego are still joined like Siamese twins—at least in awareness. No matter how much trouble your false self has caused you, it has been your meaning in the world.

You have worked hard to make your present-day experience consistent with earlier experiences. You have kept your ego intact, "happy" and safe from any potential shocks that might cause its shell to crumble.

To argue the ego away is absurd. While you may not consciously remember how your ego was formed, on occasion you might recognize how you continue to behave in ways that reinforce this definition of your false self.

It is difficult to fight with your own memories. What you remember becomes "proof" of the rightness of the definitions imposed upon you by others, and is the basis of self-fulfilling prophecy. Even your attempts to be different than what you are "prove" that something *"is"* wrong with you. Why else would you need to pretend to be someone other than who you are? Why else would you keep your SECRET YOU shamefully hidden?

No matter what you did when you were an infant, child or adolescent, *the labels—along with the feelings triggered by those labels—are the foundation of the ego.* Sadly, these learned labels are often used self-referentially—a child or teen who is told that she is stupid will often grow into an adult who calls herself "stupid." These learned labels become your meaning or role in the world.

Young minds are easily trained to confuse statements about their behavior with statements about self. What a child "does" is confused with who the child "is." For example, a parental figure might say: "Don't spill your milk, it is wasteful." Such statements are typical in child-rearing and usually won't cause harm.

However, if the parental figure says, "Don't spill your milk! You're a slob," the child will learn to associate her behavior with her self. If this happens frequently, which it often does, the child will begin to believe that she is "bad" because she is still awkward and occasionally spills things. She may also associate all "don'ts" or criticisms with being bad. Guilt and shame ensues when a child associates himself with his behavior.

Likewise, "Those are excellent grades" won't necessarily become an ego statement unless it is conveyed that you are "good" because you get good grades. In that case you learn to associate praise with *being* "good." This can lead to high anxiety due to the drive to be an over-achiever. This type of ego-training is so strong in some cultures that students may commit suicide rather than suffer the shame of a "C" grade.

But whether you have learned to refer to yourself as "good" or "bad" isn't the point. (Although, if you think of yourself as "good," it is doubtful you would be reading this book.)

The important thing about self-referential and core definitions is that they are *someone else's definitions and conclusions.* And you've been misled to believe they are true. How you define your essential being or ego has been created by others.

*To rid your self of this ego means to rid yourself of the positive **as well as** the negative concepts that define you. There is no either/or in this matter.* This can be a huge problem for some. Who in their right mind wants to rid herself of the "good" aspects of self? Nevertheless, it is necessary. A neurotic wishing to get rid of his neurotic pain cannot cling to ANY neurotic habits, even if some of those habits might make him a better artist.

Likewise, if you wish to be FREE of your false self and move past your subconscious limitations, you must UN-DO your WHOLE self, not just the aspects that you perceive as negative.

This brings us to another point—inconsistent definitions and context definitions.

Imagine a child being labeled "good" when he hits his sister. Why? Because the labeler—perhaps a step-brother—hates the girl. Yet the same act is labeled "bad" when the person hits a classmate at school. Interesting problem! The child senses that the actions were the same, the result on the "victim" the same (crying), but the response differs. So does he conclude that "meanness" is OK in some situations and not in others? Or does he conclude that he is "good" when hitting someone his step-brother dislikes, but "bad" when he hits classmates?

How does a young child understand this behavior in relation to his portrait of himself? This is a simple example, of course and in real life things can be much more confusing.

An example: Mary is labeled a "good girl" when she sits quietly, forgoes any self-pleasure and never makes a mess. What behavior is Mary learning? Can you predict that she will have problems achieving orgasm when she grows into womanhood?

Or: John is a "good boy" only when his mother is not upset, which is rare. When she isn't upset, she showers him with love... but when she is upset... So, John walks on eggshells when he is around his mom, and keeps all his problems to himself. Do you imagine that John will continue to leave his home and wife every morning at nine, and return every evening at five, even though he was laid off five months ago?

———•◦•———

Another factor in "ego development" involves "contracts" that you make with your self. Such contracts can be secretive, silent or made in public. Maybe you swear to yourself that "I'll never be deceived again...*no matter what!*" Or you make a New Year's resolution that, "I'll show the world what I'm really made of." Most self-statements of this kind are made in reaction to the pain and inadequacy caused by the metaphysical labels imposed on us.

———•◦•———

We live in a nightmare of revolving mirrors. And still, many psychologists aim to help their clients "fit in" and feel "normal." It is interesting to note that one of today's most popular drugs—Prozac—is described by some of its users as "making them feel more normal than they did prior to taking the drug." The salient question here is: Normal in relation to what?

Ego As "Evil"

To be "egotistical" is not the same as being "selfish"—though both are considered to be negative character traits by many.

Societies built upon Judeo-Christian ethical systems suggest that people should strive to be egoless and humble, and put others before self. (Much of this is based on the Golden Rule: "Love your neighbor as you love yourself"—which "good neighbors" often take as a green light to interfere in anyone's life and can lead to such horrors as "witch" burnings, holocausts, etc. After all, if you hate yourself and believe you are evil, what else can you expect as you follow the rule to "love your neighbor as you love yourself"?)

Buddhist cultures also extol the negation of the ego-self, although the emphasis is not to deny the self to serve "god," but rather to attain "enlightenment."

<hr/>

Many "ego-less" people are very weak-minded and sheep-like and are often self-destructive and destructive to their friends and family.

The weaker you are, the more you need someone to do what you are unable to do—or do not wish to do. For example, I had a friend who was a Buddhist and who wanted just to "be." In other words, he decided that because he didn't want to feed his ego, he would not work or support himself. He found a wife to do that for him while he meditated all day.

However, this case is not typical, for this person *chose* to be "ego-less," and his wife *chose* to enable him so she could feel needed and secure. Most people do not "choose" to have small or broken egos: their egos were decimated by others, usually when they were children.

Many people who grew up with parents who labeled them as "selfish" (because they were not what the parent wanted them to be) ended up with broken, weak or small egos. They subsequently suffer from what is commonly called low self-esteem, rather than selflessness or ego-death.

They are often hypersensitive and need others to do for them, as they feel too weak to speak or act for themselves.

Many "selfless" or "ego-less" people become psychological killers who interfere with the lives of others—since they have no lives of their own. As parents and teachers they destroy young genius, crushing the seed of burgeoning creative imagination. Through pity and self-hatred, such people castrate those whose value and creativity exceeds their own.

The "Good" Ego:
Ego as Authentic Self

Certain schools of thought define the Ego as the Self. That's Ego with a capital "E" and Self with a capital "S". The words may be used interchangeably in such cases.

For these folk, Ego refers to one's *authentic* and *organic* nature, rather than one's learned or false self—which you are working hard to un-do. The authentic Self is more difficult to define, primarily because it is mutable and responds to circumstances. The authentic Self or Ego remains both liquid and consistent.

The ego with a small "e" often covers or distorts your authentic Self. However, if your Authentic Self (Ego with capital "E") is killed, you probably will go insane—or die. There is a big difference between "ego" and "Ego"!

When the false personality or ego is killed, you may feel frightened, confused and anxious due to being on unfamiliar ground, but once you get accustomed to living in the present and responding to circumstances without the chains of your false self, you will feel a Lightness of Being. You will cease wondering whether you are good or bad. You will respond authentically to your loved ones and colleagues, and feel GROUNDED, be relieved of the burden of constant free-floating anxiety and tension, and feel whole and integral for perhaps the first time in your conscious memory. You will be FREE!

There is a *huge* difference between being weighted down by the albatross of your false self or little tyrant ego and living freely as your authentic Self and Natural Ego. You might even start singing like Bob Marley, Reggae legend and Rastafarian, rather than Jacob Marley, the ghost chained by the guilt and shame of his past in Dickens' *A Christmas Carol*. Bob Marley's ghost is likely resting in peace with a doobie, a guitar, and a thousand friends; Jacob Marley's ghost is tortured by chains as he stalks his ex-business partner.

Who would you rather be?

Even so, you might have to give up something for authenticity.

Sadly, your family and friends—some of whom are responsible for creating your false ego—may be overly ATTACHED to you as an anxious, miserable person. They don't want you to be your authentic self. Your misery might have made them feel that they are better off than you. Or they simply do not want you to change because they fear that you might leave them behind to suffer alone. In fact, you might find that your friends and colleagues feel so uncomfortable with the Lightness of your Being, joyfulness, and PRESENT-NESS, that they might even shun you. ("Uh-oh! He's aware! He might SEE me as the miserable asshole I really am. Time to cut a severance check before he steals my job because he has so much energy and creativity!")

This can be a pitfall for those who've worked hard to shed the false ego. Unfortunately, in a pathological society full of misery, greed and depression, FREE, CALM PEOPLE aren't usually elected to office. Society is formulated to serve the pathology of the masses, people who are chained by their egos, who have been raised to fit in society as "cogs" in the Big Wheel of Civilization.

The authentic Self can never serve as a Cog in our mechanical, dead society. The Self lives to be Itself, to respond naturally to others and Its environment, no matter the threat from those who desire to control or enslave It. The authentic Self is what causes people to act in ways that may lead to conscious martyrdom. People living life authentically often become heroes or saints, whether known to only a few or worldwide. Being near a truly authentic Soul always is a memorable experience, for such people are RARE.

The Self is like an acorn that grows to be an oak tree—even if it is planted in a coniferous forest. *The authentic Self is LIFE!*

However, most people are so polluted by their false ego that their authentic Self is submerged. Others have never had the opportunity to cultivate their authentic Selves, and find that when they do, their Self is so weak that they give up. They have no sparkle in their eyes. Such people have given up on life and are literally the walking dead. It is no wonder that so many films these days are about Zombies: *We are a civilization of Zombies.*

The authentic or organic Self is hard to define. It is that certain *je ne c'est quoi* ("I don't know what") that might be described as a twinkling in the eyes, charisma, or the feeling that this person really CARES about how you are. Or, simply, LOVE.

It can't be defined because ego or false self references are relational and reflective. To define the authentic Self is to put a cage on something that is way too wild and alive to be tamed, caught or put in a zoo. The only way to shut up an Authentic Person is to kill him or put her in exile.

⊰◈⊱

A final warning for those who are living and/or cultivating their authentic Selves:

Life is full of challenges. Without challenges, where would the fun be? Just because you finally shed your false self doesn't mean it's dead for good. The false self or ego can rise from the dead like a psychotic in a horror movie.

When the ego is overwhelmed with forces from the Self, the ego will want to inflate itself.

> DO NOT BE ALARMED IF YOU FIND YOUR AUTHENTIC SELF OCCASIONALLY SWARMED WITH SELF-APPRECIATION!

This type of ego inflation is not damaging to your authentic Self. For example, perhaps you've suffered from anorexia due to the shame that your false self caused you, but now you can look in the mirror and LIKE yourself. You might even smile at yourself, rather than avoiding mirrors like the plague.

Your ego is simply taking credit for the genes that made you beautiful. This sense of ego inflation is simply personalizing the impersonal. Often this type of inflation is natural and even necessary during the process of spiritual development.

Unless you find yourself falling into self-defeating habits that stem from insecurity, panic, fear or anxiety, do not worry. It's okay to indulge your ego once in a while. This is very different from infantile "megalomania" which is sometimes carried into adulthood as a compensation for feelings of inferiority.

WESTERN MEDITATION

Utilizing traditional Yogic methods as a form of psychotherapy is a denigration of the Yogic tradition. Yoga is a spiritual tradition with its own history and purposes. Yet some Westerners have strung the word "psychotherapy" behind the word Yoga.

If "Yoga Psychotherapy" becomes recognized as a treatment for illness in the West, then it will eventually fall under the domain of State regulation. Still, I (Hyatt), and others, have been guilty of associating some Yogic techniques with psychotherapy and, for myself, I apologize. What can we say: Yoga does what it does and it can be very useful in breaking down Body-Mind habits through breath, body-work, chanting and other methods.

Since the early 1900s, Masters of Eastern healing practices have flooded the West to teach their methods of healing and meditation. Some teachers even adopted aspects of Western religious belief systems and values—even the pathology model—to gain followers who might not be able to comprehend their methods. This was most often done as a means to an end. Their goal was acceptance and success.

One Master who rejected the Western model of pathology was Bhagwan Shree Rajneesh (Osho). Rajneesh attacked the value system and philosophy of the West which, in his view, contributed to human distress. For this he was deported from the United States and, some believe, murdered.

Most Masters of Eastern healing have been less radical and have fared better. Some of the most successful have championed one of the least threatening aspects of yoga: physical or Hatha Yoga. However, Yoga has many branches, and it is often difficult for Westerners to comprehend the branches that deal with freeing the mind, love, purification from false self and harmful behavior, etc.

Western Meditation techniques are very helpful for, well, Westerners, simply because we can understand them. The terms are written in our language.

Of course, Western Meditation has the same goal as Eastern schools. The only difference is that a Westerner developed that particular method of meditation to suit the needs of the culture.

In reality, meditation knows no geography. People have used meditation since the advent of written history, and probably earlier.

Perhaps meditation resulted as the need to be still during times of danger. Rather than simply fleeing or fighting, people discovered how to be still. After a while they began to observe other benefits from this form of self-control.

Whatever the reason, practitioners began to observe the benefits of this form of self-discipline: Peace of mind, freedom from chronic tension, pain relief via the release of natural endorphins, compassion, euphoria, happiness, a sense of purpose, enlightenment, union with the God, freedom from addictions, creativity, adding another tool to your own psychotherapy practice, getting rid of post-traumatic stress disorders, grief, or pain, etc. The list goes on.

Western Meditation as taught by Dr. Hyatt is a useful tool that works! All you have to do is DO IT!

Hyatt's methods are an advanced form of Energized Meditation and it is important that you become familiar with the fundamentals. They were first introduced in the book *Undoing Yourself with Energized Meditation and Other Devices* and are more thoroughly demonstrated in the *Radical Undoing* video series.

It is also advisable that you have some familiarity with breathing techniques and concentration methods. If you already feel confident in your knowledge, proceed. If not, practice the exercises in *Undoing Yourself,* or learn how to breath properly and concentrate using someone else's method. (The meditation books by Osho/Rajneesh also contain numerous useful methods.)

Where is God in Meditation? The God-Test

The answer is simple: God is wherever you want Him or Her to be. If you would like to discover more about your own perceptions of God, take the "God-Test" below.

While the theory and practice of meditation doesn't require a belief in God, most people have some relationship with the Numinous, whether you call yourself a Buddhist, a Neo-Pagan, or a Twelve Stepper. (I knew a man who considered himself an atheist, but viewed his Rolex watch as a higher power.) A relationship to something larger than ourselves appears to be a fundamental need of most humans. Thus, pondering your relationship to the Numinous can be enlightening. The "God-Test" may help you sort out your feelings towards the Numinous.

The Numinous and You

History often records the spirit of a person by the way he defines the Numinous. In our own lives we might understand a person by the way he lives his life in relation to God.

These assertions rest on the assumption that a relationship with the Numinous is a *primary* need, not simply for protection or utilitarian needs or even to put "meaning" into our lives, but for the "feeling of life" itself. Without the Numinous—whether it is called "God(s)" or "the Great Mystery" or "the wildcard"—life loses much of its beauty and excitement.

If everything in the Universe could be known or controlled, man could no longer exist as we know him. Thus, to know a person's nature, we simply must ask how she defines the Numinous and how she lives in relationship to these definitions. Thus, the God(s) of every culture, like the God(s) of every human, are a sign of its strength or weakness. You can learn a lot about a people from its Gods. For example, compare the Jesus of Hispanic peoples with the Jesus of a strict Protestant. The former is often depicted as an infant or a child healer, while the latter is usually depicted as an emaciated man suffering on the cross.

Often the images or symbols of the Numinous require change when society changes. Dead religion and dogma is evident when a culture refuses to let its Gods change clothes or personality. The symbol or the image is not a "thing-in-itself," but simply "channels" or sets of "channels" toward the Numinous.

Symbols and images are simply what the "rational mind" can comprehend. Religious or mythological images function as a conduit between our selves and the Numinous. Choose the symbols and images you surround yourself with wisely.

By definition, the Numinous can't be dissected or known by reductive means. Science, of course, uses reductive methods, and thus cannot deal with the mystery of the Numinous—to the dismay of some Romantic poets who accuse science of dissecting, and thus ruining, the beauty of a rainbow. But such criticism has not made its way to religion even though most Religions are as reductive in their means as Science: they reduce the Numinous to a *single vision* and propagate that single vision to the masses.

When the appeal to the Numinous is only through the dogma of a Religion, the Mystery, the ineffability, and the magic is lost. When dogmas have worn thin and the metaphors of a sacred text have laid down and died, so does the appearance of the Numinous. When this happens politicians control theology and mystics are burned as heretics. The Numinous crawls into a cave and people wonder "Where is God? Why doesn't She help the world?"

The understanding given to us by science or by religious dogma, while helping us to live more convenient lives, can never contain the essential truth of the mystical and the Numinous.

The God-Test

Examine three forms of the Numinous: The God of the Judeo-Christian-Muslim tradition, the Gods of Africa, and Dionysus, a God of the early Greeks.

We will use a series of seven-point scales to give us our results.

Rate the Judeo-Christian-Muslim God:

Strong — — — — — — — Weak   **Doesn't apply —

Orderly — — — — — — — Chaotic **Doesn't apply —

Lustful — — — — — — — Chaste **Doesn't apply —

Is this God primarily forgiving, vengeful or indifferent toward man? Choose one.

Now rate the image of a human as this God sees him.

Strong — — — — — — — Weak   **Doesn't apply —

Orderly — — — — — — — Chaotic **Doesn't apply —

Lustful — — — — — — — Chaste **Doesn't apply —

Now rate the African Gods:

Strong — — — — — — — Weak   **Doesn't apply —

Orderly — — — — — — — Chaotic **Doesn't apply —

Lustful — — — — — — — Chaste **Doesn't apply —

Are these Gods primarily forgiving, vengeful or indifferent toward humans? Choose one.

Now rate the image of humans as these Gods see him:

Strong — — — — — — — Weak   **Doesn't apply —

Orderly — — — — — — — Chaotic **Doesn't apply —

Lustful — — — — — — — Chaste **Doesn't apply —

Rate the God Dionysus:

Strong — — — — — — — Weak   **Doesn't apply —

Orderly — — — — — — — Chaotic **Doesn't apply —

Lustful — — — — — — — Chaste **Doesn't apply —

Is this God primarily forgiving, vengeful or indifferent toward humans? Choose one.

Now rate the image of humans as Dionysus sees him:

Strong — — — — — — — Weak   **Doesn't apply —

Orderly — — — — — — — Chaotic **Doesn't apply —

Lustful — — — — — — — Chaste **Doesn't apply —

Repeat this test with Buddha, Satan and Nietzsche's hero Zarathustra.

Rate the God ___.

Strong — — — — — — — Weak   **Doesn't apply —

Orderly — — — — — — — Chaotic **Doesn't apply —

Lustful — — — — — — — Chaste **Doesn't apply —

Is this God primarily forgiving, vengeful or indifferent toward humans? Choose one.

Now rate the image of humans as ___ sees him.

Strong — — — — — — — Weak   **Doesn't apply —

Orderly — — — — — — — Chaotic **Doesn't apply —

Lustful — — — — — — — Chaste **Doesn't apply —

Try This Now!!!

When you have completed your ratings, write a short paragraph describing the relationship between man and his Gods. How similar are they? How different are they?

Finally, and most importantly, define *your* concept of God (vision of the Numinous) and rate Him or Her. Also rate how this God "sees" you.

This method will provide you with a map of how a culture—or a man—perceives himself in relation to the Numinous. It will also allow you to make predictions about how a man or a culture will change over time. More importantly it will guide you towards initiating a real personal relationship with your own personal GOD.

DEVOTION

Bhakti Yoga, or "devotion," is one of the most powerful methods of empowering and filling yourself with passion. Once you have added Body-Mind meditation techniques to rid your self of all remnants of the false self and connect you to the Numinous, the results of devotional yoga can be overpowering. Some might say this is because the "chakras" have been opened and true spiritual intercourse can now occur between the devotee and God.

The article below was written by Aleister Crowley. (Now, lest you feel tempted to put this book down, you don't have to like or accept Mr. Crowley to take advantage of his brilliance or his experiences. Crowley's genius and knowledge have been lost to too many who have thrown the baby out with the bathwater.)

While this article contains many terms and names with which you might not be familiar, do not let this stop you from benefiting from the insights of this Rascal Mage.

Liber Astarte

0. This is the book of Uniting Himself to a particular Deity by devotion.

1. *Considerations before the Threshold.* First, concerning the choice of a particular Deity. This matter is of no import, sobeit that thou choose one suited to thine own highest nature. Howsoever, this method is not so suitable for gods austere as Saturn, or intellectual as Thoth. But for such deities as in themselves partake in anywise of love it is a perfect mode.

2. *Concerning the prime method of this Magick Art.* Let the devotee consider well that although Christ and Osiris be one, yet the former is to be worshipped with Christian, and the latter with Egyptian rites. And this although the rites themselves are ceremonially equivalent. There should, however, be *one* symbol declaring the transcending of such limitations; and with regard to the Deity also, there should be some *one* affirmation of his identity

both with all other similar gods of other nations, and with the Supreme of whom all are but partial reflections.

3. *Concerning the chief place of devotion.* This is the Heart of the devotee, and should be symbolically represented by that room or spot which he loves best. And the dearest spot therein shall be the shrine of his temple. It is most convenient if this shrine and altar should be sequestered in woods, or in a private grove, or garden. But let it be protected from the profane.

4. *Concerning the Image of the Deity.* Let there be an image of the Deity; first, because in meditation there is mindfulness induced thereby; and second, because a certain power enters and inhabits it by virtue of the ceremonies; or so it is said, and We deny it not. Let this image be the most beautiful and perfect which the devotee is able to procure; or if he be able to paint or to carve the same, it is all the better. As for Deities with whose nature no Image is compatible, let them be worshipped in an empty shrine. Such are Brahma and Allah. Also some post-captivity conceptions of Jehovah.

5. *Further concerning the shrine.* Let this shrine be furnished appropriately as to its ornaments, according to the book 777. With ivy and pine-cones, that is to say, for Bacchus, and let lay before him both grapes and wine. So also for Ceres let there be corn, and cakes; or for Diana moon-wort and pale herbs, and pure water. Further, it is well to support the shrine with talismans of the planets, signs and elements appropriate. But these should be made according to the right Ingenium of the Philosophus by the light of the book 777 during the course of his Devotion. It is also well, nevertheless, if a magick circle with the right signs and names be made beforehand.

6. *Concerning the ceremonies.* Let the Philosophus prepare a powerful Invocation of the particular Deity, according to his Ingenium. But let it consist of these several parts:

First, an Imprecation, as of a slave unto his Lord.
Second, an Oath, as of a vassal to his Liege.
Third, a Memorial, as of a child to his Parent.
Fourth, an Orison, as of a Priest unto his God.
Fifth, a Colloquy, as of a Brother with his Brother.
Sixth, a Conjuration, as of a Friend with his Friend.
Seventh, a Madrigal, as of a Lover to his Mistress.

And mark well that the first should be of awe, the second of fealty, the third of dependence, the fourth of adoration, the fifth of confidence, the sixth of comradeship, the seventh of passion.

7. *Further concerning the ceremonies.* Let then this Invocation be the principal part of an ordered ceremony. And in this ceremony let the Philosophus in no wise neglect the service of a menial. Let him sweep and garnish the place, sprinkling it with water or with wine as is appropriate to the particular Deity, and consecrating it with oil, and with such ritual as may seem him best. And let all be done with intensity and minuteness.

8. *Concerning the period of devotion, and the hours thereof.* Let a fixed period be set for the worship; and it is said that the least time is nine days by seven, and the greatest seven years by nine. And concerning the hours, let the Ceremony be performed every day thrice, or at least once, and let the sleep of the Philosophus be broken for some purpose of devotion at least once in every night.

Now to some it may seem best to appoint fixed hours for the ceremony, to others it may seem that the ceremony should be performed as the spirit moves them so to do: for this there is no rule.

9. *Concerning the Robes and Instruments.* The Wand and Cup are to be chosen for this Art; never the Sword or Dagger, never the Pantacle, unless that Pantacle chance to be of a nature harmonious. But even so it is best to keep the Wand and Cup; and if one must choose, the Cup.

For the Robes, that of a Philosophus, or that of an Adept Within is most suitable; or, the robe best fitted for the service of the particular Deity, as a bassara for Bacchus, a white robe for Vesta. So also, for Vesta, one might use for an instrument the Lamp; or the sickle, for Chronos.

10. *Concerning the Incense and Libations.* The incense should follow the nature of the particular Deity; as, mastic for Mercury, dittany for Persephone. Also the libations, as, a decoction of nightshade for Melancholia, or of Indian hemp for Uranus.

11. *Concerning the harmony of the ceremonies.* Let all these things be rightly considered, and at length, in language of the utmost beauty at the command of the Philosophus, accompanied, if he have skill, by music, and interwoven, if the particular Deity be jocund, with dancing. And all being carefully prepared and

rehearsed, let it be practised daily until it be wholly rhythmical with his aspiration, and as it were, a part of his being.

12. *Concerning the variety of the ceremonies.* Now, seeing that every man differeth essentially from every other man, albeit in essence he is identical, let also these ceremonies assert their identity by their diversity. For this reason do We leave much herein to the right Ingenium of the Philosophus.

13. *Concerning the life of the devotee.* First, let his way of life be such as is pleasing to the particular Deity. Thus to invoke Neptune, let him go a-fishing; but if Hades, let him not approach the water that is hateful to Him.

14. *Further, concerning the life of the devotee.* Let him cut away from his life any act, word, or thought, that is hateful to the particular Deity; as, unchastity in the case of Artemis, evasions in the case of Ares. Besides this, he should avoid all harshness or unkindness of any kind in thought, word, or deed, seeing that above the particular Deity is One in whom all is One. Yet also he may deliberately practise cruelties, where the particular Deity manifests His love in that manner; as in the case of Kali, and of Pan. And therefore, before the beginning of his period of devotion, let him practise according to the rules of *Liber Jugorum.*

15. *Further concerning the life of the devotee.* Now, as many are fully occupied with their affairs, let it be known that this method is adaptable to the necessities of all.
And We bear witness that this which followeth is the Crux and Quintessence of the whole Method.
First, if he have no Image, let him take anything soever, and consecrate it as an Image of his God. Likewise with his robes and instruments, his suffumigations and libations: for his Robe hath he not a night-dress; for his instrument a walking-stick; for his suffumigation a burning match, for his libation a glass of water?
But let him consecrate each thing that he useth to the service of that particular Deity, and not profane the same to any other use.

16. *Continuation.* Next, concerning his time, if it be short. Let him labour mentally upon his Invocation, concentrating it, and let him perform this Invocation in his heart whenever he hath the leisure. And let him seize eagerly upon every opportunity for this.

17. *Continuation.* Third, even if he have leisure and preparation, let him seek ever to bring inward the symbols, so that even in his well-ordered shrine the whole ceremony revolve inwardly in his heart, that is to say in the temple of his body, of which the outer temple is but an image.

For in the brain is the shrine, and there is no Image therein; and the breath of man is the incense and the libation.

18. *Continuation.* Further concerning occupation. Let the devotee transmute within the alembic of his heart every thought, or word, or act into the spiritual gold of his devotion.

As thus: eating. Let him say: "I eat this food in gratitude to my Deity that hath sent it to me, in order to gain strength for my devotion to Him."

Or: sleeping. Let him say: "I lie down to sleep, giving thanks for this blessing from my Deity, in order that I may be refreshed for new devotion to Him."

Or: reading. Let him say: "I read this book that I may study the nature of my Deity, that further knowledge of Him may inspire me with deeper devotion to Him."

Or: working. Let him say: "I drive my spade into the earth that fresh flowers (fruit, or what not) may spring up to His glory, and that I, purified by toil, may give better devotion to Him."

Or, whatever it may be that he is doing, let him reason it out in his own mind, drawing it through circumstance and circumstance to that one end and conclusion of the matter. And let him not perform the act until he hath done this.

As it is written: *Liber* VII, cap. v:

> 22. Every breath, every word, every thought, is an act of love with thee.
> 23. The beat of my heart is the pendulum of love.
> 24. The songs of me are the soft sighs:
> 25. The thoughts of me are very rapture:
> 26. And my deeds are the myriads of Thy children, the stars and the atoms.

And Remember Well, that if thou wert in truth a lover, all this wouldst thou do of thine own nature without the slightest flaw or failure in the minutest part thereof.

19. *Concerning the Lections.* Let the Philosophus read solely in his copies of the holy books of Thelema, during the whole period

of his devotion. But if he weary, then let him read books which have no part whatever in love, as for recreation.

But let him copy out each verse of Thelema which bears upon this matter, and ponder them, and comment thereupon. For therein is a wisdom and a magic too deep to utter in any other wise.

20. *Concerning the Meditations.* Herein is the most potent method of attaining unto the End, for him who is thoroughly prepared, being purified by the practice of the Transmutation of deed into devotion, and consecrated by the right performance of the holy ceremonies. Yet herein is danger, for that the Mind is fluid as quicksilver, and bordereth upon the Abyss, and is beset by many sirens and devils that seduce and attack it to destroy it. Therefore let the devotee beware, and precise accurately his meditations, even as a man should build a canal from sea to sea.

21. *Continuation.* Let then the Philosophus meditate upon all love that hath ever stirred him. There is the love of David and of Jonathan, and the love of Abraham and Isaac, and the love of Lear and Cordelia, and the love of Damon and Pythias, and the love of Sappho and Atthis, and the love of Romeo and Juliet, and the love of Dante and Beatrice, and the love of Paolo and Francesca, and the love of Caesar and Lucrezia Borgia, and the love of Aucassin and Nicolette, and the love of Daphnis and Chloe, and the love of Cornelia and Caius Gracchus, and the love of Bacchus and Ariadne, and the love of Cupid and Psyche, and the love of Endymion and Artemis, and the love of Demeter and Persephone, and the love of Venus and Adonis, and the love of Lakshmi and Vishnu, and the love of Siva and Bhavani, and the love of Buddha and Ananda, and the love of Jesus and John, and many more.

Also there is the love of many saints for their particular deity, as of St Francis of Assisi for Christ, of Sri Sabhapaty Swami for Maheswara, of Abdullah Haji Shirazi for Allah, of St Ignatius Loyola for Mary, and many more.

Now do thou take one such story every night, and enact it in thy mind, grasping each identity with infinite care and zest, and do thou figure thyself as one of the lovers and thy Deity as the other. Thus do thou pass through all adventures of love, not omitting one; and to each do thou conclude: How pale a reflection is this of my love for this Deity!

Yet from each shalt thou draw some knowledge of love, some intimacy with love, that shall aid thee to perfect thy love. Thus learn the humility of love from one, its obedience from another, its intensity from a third, its purity from a fourth, its peace from yet a fifth.

So then thy love being made perfect, it shall be worthy of that perfect love of His.

22. *Further concerning meditation.* Moreover, let the Philosophus imagine to himself that he hath indeed succeeded in his devotion, and that his Lord hath appeared to him, and that they converse as may be fitting.

23. *Concerning the Mysterious Triangle.* Now then as three cords separately may be broken by a child, while those same cords duly twisted may bind a giant, let the Philosophus learn to entwine these three methods of Magic into a Spell.

To this end let him understand that as they are One, because the end is one, so are they One because the method is One, even the method of turning the mind toward the particular Deity by love in every act.

And lest thy twine slip, here is a little cord that wrappeth tightly round and round all, even the Mantram or Continuous Prayer.

24. *Concerning the Mantram or Continuous Prayer.* Let the Philosophus weave the Name of the Particular Deity into a sentence short and rhythmical; as, for Artemis: [Greek] epsilon-pi-epsilon-lambda-theta-omicron-nu, epsilon-pi-epsilon-lambda-theta-omicron-nu, Alpha-rho-tau-epsilon-mu-iota-sigma; or, for Shiva: Namo Shivaya namaha Aum; or, for Mary: [Latin] Ave Maria; or for Pan, [Greek] chi-alpha-iota-rho-epsilon-pi Sigma-omega-tau-eta-rho kappa-omicron-sigma-mu-omicron-upsilon, Iota-omega Pi-alpha-nu, Iota-omega Pi-alpha-nu; or, for Allah: [Arabic] Hua Allahu alazi lailaha illa Hua.

Let him repeat this day and night without cessation mechanically in his brain, which is thus made ready for the Advent of that Lord, and armed against all other.

25. *Concerning the Active and the Passive.* Let the Philosophus change from the active love of his particular Deity to a state of passive awaiting, even almost a repulsion, the repulsion not of distaste, but of a sublime modesty.

As it is written, *Liber LXV, ii:* 59: "I have called unto Thee, and I have journeyed unto Thee, and it availed me not." 60: "I waited patiently, and Thou wast with me from the beginning."

Then let him change back to the Active, until a veritable rhythm is established between the states, as it were the swinging of a Pendulum. But let him reflect that a vast intelligence is required for this; for he must stand as it were almost without himself to watch those phases of himself. And to do this is a high Art, and pertaineth not altogether to the grade of Philosophus. Neither is it of itself helpful, but rather the reverse, in this especial practice.

26. *Concerning Silence.* Now there may come a time in the course of this practice when the outward symbols of devotion cease, when the soul is as it were dumb in the presence of its God. Mark that this is not a cessation, but a transmutation of the barren seed of prayer into the green shoot of yearning. This yearning is spontaneous, and it shall be left to grow, whether it be sweet or bitter. For often times it is as the torment of hell in which the soul burns and writhes unceasingly. Yet it ends, and at its end continue openly thy Method.

27. *Concerning Dryness.* Another state wherein at times the soul may fall is this dark night. And this is indeed purifying in such depths that the soul cannot fathom it. It is less like pain than like death. But it is the necessary death that comes before the rising of a body glorified.

This state must be endured with fortitude; and no means of alleviating it may be employed. It may be broken up by the breaking up of the whole Method, and a return to the world without. This cowardice not only destroys the value of all that has gone before, but destroys the value of the Oath of Fealty that thou hast sworn, and makes thy Will a mockery to men and gods.

28. *Concerning the Deceptions of the Devil.* Note well that in this state of dryness a thousand seductions will lure thee away; also a thousand means of breaking thine oath in spirit without breaking it in letter. Against this thou mayst repeat the words of thine oath aloud again and again until the temptation be overcome.

Also the devil will represent to thee that it were much better for this operation that thou do thus and thus, and seek to affright thee by fears for thy health or thy reason.

Or he may send against thee visions worse than madness.

Against all this there is but one remedy, the Discipline of thine Oath. So then thou shalt go through ceremonies meaningless and hideous to thee, and blaspheme shalt thou against thy Deity and curse Him. And this mattereth little, for it is not thou, so be that thou adhere to the Letter of thine Obligation. For thy Spiritual Sight is closed, and to trust it is to be led unto the precipice, and hurled therefrom.

29. *Further of this matter.* Now also subtler than all these terrors are the Illusions of Success. For one instant's self-satisfaction or Expansion of thy Spirit, especially in this state of dryness, and thou art lost. For thou mayst attain the False Union with the Demon himself. Beware also of even the pride which rises from having resisted the temptations.

But so many and so subtle are the wiles of Choronzon that the whole world could not contain their enumeration.

The answer to one and all is the persistence in the literal fulfillment of the routine. Beware, then, last, of that devil who shall whisper in thine ear that the letter killeth, but the spirit giveth life, and answer: Except a corn of wheat fall into the ground and die, it abideth alone; but if it die, it bringeth forth much fruit.

Yet shalt thou also beware of disputation with the devil, and pride in the cleverness of thine answers to him. Therefore, if thou hast not lost the power of silence, let it be first and last employed against him.

30. *Concerning the Enflaming of the Heart.* Now learn that thy methods are dry one and all. Intellectual exercises, moral exercises, they are not Love. Yet as a man, rubbing two dry sticks together for long, suddenly found a spark, so also from time to time will true love leap unasked into thy meditation. Yet this shall die and be reborn again and again. It may be that thou hast no tinder near.

In the end shall come suddenly a great flame and a devouring, and burn thee utterly.

Now of these sparks, and of these splutterings of flame, and of these beginnings of the Infinite Fire, thou shalt thus be aware. For the sparks thy heart shall leap up, and thy ceremony or meditation or toil shall seem of a sudden to go of its own will; and for the little flames this shall be increased in volume and intensity; and for the beginnings of the Infinite Fire thy ceremony shall be caught up unto ravishing song, and thy meditation shall ecstasy, and thy toil shall be a delight exceeding all pleasure thou hast ever known.

And of the Great Flame that answereth thee it may not be spoken; for therein is the End of this Magick Art Devotion.

31. *Considerations with regard to the use of symbols.* It to be noted that persons of powerful imagination, will, and intelligence have no need of these material symbols. There have been certain saints who are capable of love for an idea as such without it being otherwise than deaded by *idolising* it, to use this word in its true sense. Thus one may be impassioned of beauty, without even the need of so small a concretion of it as "the beauty of Apollo," "the beauty of roses," "the beauty of Attis." Such persons are rare; it may be doubted whether Plato himself attained to any vision of absolute beauty without attaching to it material objects in the first place. A second class is able to contemplate ideals through this veil; a third class need a double veil, and cannot think of the beauty of a rose without a rose before them. For such is Method of most use; yet let them know that there is this danger therein, that they may mistake the gross body the symbol for the idea made concrete thereby.

32. *Considerations of further danger to those not purged material thought.* Let it be remembered that in the nature the love itself is danger. The lust of the satyr for the nymph is indeed of the same nature as the affinity of quicklime for water on the one hand, and of the love of Ab for Ama on the other; so also is the triad Osiris, Isis, Horus like that of a horse, mare, foal, and of red, blue, purple. And this is the foundation of Correspondences.

But it were false to say "Horus is a foal" or "Horus is purple." One may say "Horus resembles a foal in this respect, that he is the offspring of two complementary beings."

33. *Further of this matter. So* also many have said truly that all is one, and falsely that since earth is That One, and ocean is That One, therefore earth is ocean. Unto Him good is illusion, and evil is illusion; therefore good is evil. By this fallacy of logic are many men destroyed.

Moreover, there are those who take the image for the God; as who should say, my heart is in Tiphereth, and an Adeptus is in Tiphereth; I am therefore an adept.

And in this practice the worst danger is this, that the love which is its weapon should fail in one of two ways.

First, if the love lack any quality of love, so long is it not ideal love. For it is written of the Perfected One: "There is no member of my body which is not the member of some god." Therefore let not the Philosophus despise any form of love, but harmonize all. As it is written, *Liber LXI, 32:* "So therefore Perfection abideth not in the Pinnacles or in the Foundation, but in the harmony of One with all."

Second, if any part of this love exceed, there is disease therein. As, in the love of Othello for Desdemona, love's jealousy overcame love's tenderness, so may it be in this love of a particular Deity. And this is more likely, since in this divine love no element may be omitted.

It is by virtue of this completeness that no human love may in any way attain to more than to forthshadow a little part thereof.

34. *Concerning Mortifications.* These are not necessary to this method. On the contrary, they may destroy the concentration, as counter-irritants to, and so alleviations of, the supreme mortification which is the Absence of the Deity invoked.

Yet as in mortal love arises a distaste for food, or a pleasure in things naturally painful, this perversion should be endured and allowed to take its course. Yet not to the interference with natural bodily health, whereby the instrument of the soul might be impaired.

And concerning sacrifices for love's sake, they are natural to this Method, and right.

But concerning voluntary privations and tortures, without use save as against the devotee, they are generally not natural to healthy natures, and wrong. For they are selfish. To scourge one's self serves not one's master; yet to deny one's self bread that one's child may have cake, the act of a true mother.

35. *Further concerning Mortifications.* If thy body, on which thou ridest, be so disobedient a beast that by no means will he travel in the desired direction, or if thy mind be baulkish and eloquent as Balaam's fabled Ass, then let the practice be abandoned. Let the shrine be covered in sackcloth, and do thou put on habits of lamenation, and abide alone. And do thou return most austerely to the practice of *Liber Jugorum*, testing thyself by a standard higher than that hitherto accomplished, and punishing effractions with a heavier goad. Nor do thou return to thy devotion until that body and mind are tamed and trained to all manner of peaceable going.

36. *Concerning minor methods adjuvant in the ceremonies. I. Rising on the planes.* By this method mayst thou assist the imagination at the time of concluding thine Invocation. Act as taught in *Liber 0,* by the light of *Liber 777.*

37. *Concerning minor methods adjuvant in the ceremonies. II. Talismanic magic.* Having made by thine Ingenium a talisman or pantacle to represent the particular Deity, and consecrated it with infinite love and care, do thou burn it ceremonially before the shrine, as if thereby giving up the shadow for the substance. But it is useless to do this unless thou do really in thine heart value the talisman beyond all else that thou hast.

38 *Concerning minor methods adjuvant in the ceremonies. III. Rehearsal.* It may assist if the traditional history of the particular Deity be rehearsed before him; perhaps this is best done in dramatic form. This method is the main one recommended in the *Exercitios Espirituales* of St Ignatius, whose work may be taken as a model. Let the Philosophus work out the legend of his own particular Deity, and apportioning days to events, live that life in imagination, exercising the five senses in turn, as occasion arises.

39. *Concerning minor matters adjuvant in the ceremonies. IV. Duresse.* This method consists in cursing a deity recalcitrant; as, threatening ceremonially "to burn the blood of Osiris, and to grind down his bones to powder." This method is altogether contrary to the spirit of love, unless the particular Deity be himself savage and relentless; as, Jehovah or Kali. In such a case the desire to perform constraint and cursing may be the sign of the assimilation of the spirit of the devotee with that of his God, and so an advance to the Union with Him.

40. *Concerning the value of this particular form of Union or Samadhi.* All Samadhi is defined as the ecstatic union of subject and object in consciousness, with the result that a third thing arises which partakes in no way of the nature of the two.

It would seem at first sight that it is of no importance whatever to choose an object of meditation. For example, the Samadhi called Atmadarshana might arise from simple concentration of the thought on an imagined triangle, or on the heart.

But as the union of two bodies in chemistry may be endothermic or exothermic, the combination of Oxygen with Nitrogen is gentle, while that of Oxygen with Hydrogen is explosive; and as it is found that the most heat is disengaged as a rule by the union of bodies most opposite in character, and that the compound resulting from such is most stable, so it seems reasonable to suggest that the most important and enduring Samadhi results from the contemplation of the Object most opposite to the devotee. On other planes, it has been suggested that the most opposed types make the best marriages and produce the healthiest children. The greatest pictures and operas are those in which violent extremes are blended, and so generally in every field of activity. Even in mathematics, the greatest parallelogram is formed if the lines composing it are set at right angles.

41. *Conclusions from the foregoing.* It may then be suggested to the Philosophus, that although his work will be harder his reward will be greater if he choose a Deity most remote from his own nature. This method is harder and higher than that of *Liber E.* For a simple object as there suggested is of the same nature as the commonest things of life, while even the meanest Deity is beyond uninitiated human understanding. On the same plane, too, Venus is nearer to man than Aphrodite, Aphrodite than Isis, Isis than Babalon, Babalon than Nuit.

Let him decide therefore according to his discretion on the one hand and his aspiration on the other: and let not one outrun his fellow.

42. *Further concerning the value of this Method.* Certain objections arise. Firstly, in the nature of all human love is illusion, and a certain blindness. Nor is there any true love below the Veil of the Abyss. For this reason We give this Method to the Philosophus, as the reflection of the Exempt Adept, who reflects the Magister Templi and the Magus. Let then the Philosophus attain this method as a foundation of the higher Methods to be given to him when he attains those higher grades.

Another objection lies in the partiality of this Method. This is equally a defect characteristic of the Grade.

43. *Concerning a notable danger of Success.* It may occur that owing to the tremendous power of the Samadhi, overcoming all other memories as it should and does do, that the mind of the devotee may be obsessed, so that he declare his particular Deity to be sole God and Lord. This error has been the foundation of all dogmatic religions, and so the cause of more misery than all other errors combined.

The Philosophus is peculiarly liable to this because from the nature of the Method he cannot remain sceptical; he must for the time believe in his particular Deity. But let him (1) consider that this belief is only a weapon in his hands, (2) affirm sufficiently that his Deity is but an emanation or reflection or eidolon of a Being beyond him, as was said in Paragraph 2. For if he fail herein, since man cannot remain permanently in Samadhi, the memorized Image in his mind will be degraded, and replaced by the corresponding Demon, to his utter ruin.

Therefore, after Success, let him not delight overmuch in his Deity, but rather busy himself with his other work, not permitting that which is but a step to become a goal. As it is written also, *Liber CLXXXV:* "remembering that Philosophy is the Equilibrium of him that is in the House of Love."

44. *Concerning secrecy, and the rites of Blood.* During this practice it is most wise that the Philosophus utter no word concerning his working, as if it were a Forbidden Love that consumeth him. But let him answer fools according to their folly; for since he cannot conceal his love from his fellows, he must speak to them as they may understand.

And as many Deities demand sacrifices, one of men, another of cattle, a third of doves, let these sacrifices be replaced by the true sacrifices in thine own heart. Yet if thou must symbolise them outwardly for the hardness of thine heart, let thine own blood, and not another's, be It before that altar.

Nevertheless, forget not that this practice is dangerous, and may cause the manifestation of evil things, hostile and malicious, to thy great hurt.

45. *Concerning a further sacrifice.* Of this it shall be understood that nothing is to be spoken; nor need anything be spoken to him that hath wisdom to comprehend the number of the paragraph. And this sacrifice is fatal beyond all, unless it be a *sacrificium* indeed. Yet there those who have dared and achieved thereby.

46. *Concerning yet a further sacrifice.* Here it is spoken actual mutilation. Such acts are abominable; and while they may bring success in this Method, form an absolute bar to all further progress.

And they are in any case more likely to lead to madness than to Samadhi. He indeed who purposeth them is already mad.

47. *Concerning human affection.* During this practice thou shalt in no wise withdraw thyself from human relations, only figuring to thyself that thy father or thy brother or thy wife is as it were an image of thy particular Deity. Thus shall they gain, and not lose, by thy working. Only in the case of thy wife this is difficult, since she is more to thee than all others, and in this case thou mayst: with temperance, lest her personality overcome and destroy that of thy Deity.

48. *Concerning the Holy Guardian Angel.* Do thou in no wise confuse this invocation with that.

49. *The Benediction.* And so may the Love that passeth all Understanding keep your hearts and minds through IAW ADWNAI ÇABAW and through Babalon of the City of the Pyramids, and through Astarte the Starry One green-girdled in the name Ararita.
Amen.

A Special Message For the Over Thirty Crowd

"...We age when we are no longer challenged by the dream."
— Leo Buscaglia

Only a handful of people define their talents prior to acquiring their driver's licenses; fewer still find themselves in an environment supportive of their aspirations; and even fewer enjoy liberal access to the tools and training necessary for the cultivation of their possible genius. Yet we often compare ourselves with this fortunate few when judging our own abilities. We stand in awe of Mozart, whose tiny fingers danced the keyboards at four; Picasso, who mastered drawing at ten; and even cousin Sally, whose childhood dream of becoming a doctor was fulfilled before her twenty-fourth birthday.

Most of us, however, gave little consideration to our future prospects as we floated contentedly down the myriad rivers of childhood and adolescence. We let our circumstances define us: the words of parents, peers and teachers strongly influenced the directions in which we drifted. Suddenly, we find ourselves in grown-up clothes, caught up in the daily grind. We may stop and ask, "How did I get here?" only to uncover no satisfactory answer. Yet the very act of questioning widens our perspective—a revelation may result, followed by the recognition of a latent potential, a dream long forgotten, and an overwhelming sense that anything *is* possible. Unfortunately, these fleeting moments quickly pass. Our bills seem to be cloning themselves in the mailbox and the telephone is ringing again. We have neither the time to acknowledge childhood fancies nor the energy to follow the oracle's advice and truly "know" ourselves. Our dreams remain unbloomed.

We are lawyers yearning to be teachers, teachers who'd rather be restaurateurs, accountants aching to express ourselves with oil paints, homemakers fantasizing about high-powered careers, high-powered career women fantasizing about homemaking, psychiatrists craving lives as jazz pianists, and anyone who houses a dream yet untried. Perhaps, *your* dream remains unnamed, patiently awaiting definition, and calling to you only when the moon is blue. The subtle nagging of the neglected dream may take the shape of addictive behavior, a sudden anxiety, a midnight epiphany shouting for a more meaningful life, an ongoing depression, or a sense that some mysterious geyser of creative force rests dormant within the depths of your psyche. Listen: If you quiet your mind and still your body, you will feel your dreams beckon. "Acknowledge us, nourish us, and embrace joy," they whisper.

Sustaining the dream and working toward its fulfillment is a tough enough task for anyone, and Late Bloomers, in particular, will find themselves constantly battling the dream-destroying affliction known as discouragement. Modern culture is overtly youth-oriented. The under twenty-three crowd feasts at the table of dreams, while Late Bloomers, having passed up the edibles ten years back, must now risk their egos for a scrap. Ideally, adulthood would instill us with the freedom and confidence necessary to fully grow into ourselves; more often, it simply demands that "youthful" icons of Conscious Rebellion, Risk, Energy, Creativity and Change are replaced with the more "mature" deities of Insurance, Stability, Compliance and Rootedness. In worshipping the latter pantheon, the idea of being a "grown-up" becomes a terminal condition. (No wonder Peter Pan complexes abound in modern society.)

Because stability implies safety, the Late Bloomer's anticipated metamorphosis may threaten those who feel comfortable in "knowing you like a book." Blooming heralds transformation. When loved ones tell you they love you just as you are, *they mean it.* So if you're forty-two and itching to master the art of belly dancing, learn the trombone, or resume working toward that Ph.D. in archaeology, don't be surprised if your friends don a worried expression and offer referrals to psychotherapists and marriage counselors. Change frightens most people—a familiar backyard tree cannot uproot itself and dance on the sidewalk without causing a ruckus! Assure your loved ones that while sturdy roots are fundamental to surviving typhoons, joy prefers brightly colored blossoms and the quivering leaves of wayward branches. Roots and Wings only *seem* mutually exclusive. Really.

But where loved ones and societal restrictions prove hurdles in the road to self-realization, the Late Bloomer's greatest obstacle is her own self doubt. The poet William Blake, recognizing doubt as an insidious sorcery, wrote, "If the Sun & Moon should doubt / They'd immediately Go out." Ah, but you consider yourself neither as radiant as the sun nor as mysterious as the moon, and to prove it you comprise a tall list of prerequisites which need be fulfilled before you begin attending to the dream-in-waiting. You need more time, money, talent, encouragement, hair and a house on the beach; if only you were blonder, taller, smarter, firmer, violet-eyed or shorter.

Consider the long-suffering protagonist of Charles Schulz' *Snoopy* comic strip. Every Halloween Charlie Brown receives rocks in lieu of treats. Not because he's prematurely bald, but because he's the type of kid who compels the giver to "trick" rather than "treat"—his attitude, if you will, solicits rocks. When Charlie Brown decides to stick his head out the window of his low self-esteem and shout, "I'm not gonna take it anymore," he'll get candy. Life can be likened to a huge, perpetually changing canvas. How it appears at any given moment depends on who's holding the brush. Charlie Brown has painted himself in the clothes of a loser. Unfortunately he lacks the knowledge (and confidence) to don the artist's smock and repaint himself in a happier suit.

Zen teachers create riddles called koans to impress upon their students this idea that they are the painters of their reality. "Who is the Master who makes the grass green?"

Dig deep enough into your own pockets and you'll find enough paint and brushes to keep you busy until the final sleep. That's right, the answer to the riddle is that *you* are the master; the green of the grass exists only in your head. If you don't believe me ask your dog, or a color-blind friend. As the philosopher Nietzsche once noted, "We are all greater artists than we realize."

⟫◦⟪

Defining yourself by what you do for a living is a sure way to limit your potential and sabotage your dream. Imposing labels on yourself (as if you were a can of Campbell's Soup) may cause you to buy into the idea that you *are* what you do, and dissuade you from even thinking to add tomato bisque to the cream of mushroom. It helps to think like a Hopi Indian. Because the Hopi language lacks the subject-predicate structure of Indo-European languages, it is impossible to define yourself by your job title when you're not actually on the job.

For example, a Hopi woman defines herself by what she is doing *at present,* understanding herself to be a dancer when she dances; a hunter, when hunting; a mother, when mothering; a cook, when cooking; and a poet, when creating. The Hopi people perceive themselves as being in a constant state of flux—that is, they see themselves as verbs, rather than nouns, realizing that there's more than one answer to the "Who am I" question. Danger resides in *absolute* definitions, and we all might find some personal liberation in adopting the phrase, "I am a verb" as our personal mantram. The focus is on *process,* not *product*; on journey, never destination. The dancer disappears when the dancing stops, clearing the room for the next dreamer, and another dream.

———◦◦◦———

Unfortunately, many people prefer to subscribe to age-ist notions such as "old dogs can't learn new tricks" and/or static dogmas like "rolling stones gather no moss." Late Bloomers, however, can credit themselves as being smarter than hounds and more limber than stones. Modern science proves that change is the only constant, and physiological fact informs us that our bodies rebuild themselves, cell by cell, approximately every seven years. You won't be a finished product until you're embalmed or frozen! "Today is the First Day of the Rest of Your Life" is still a worthy affirmation.

What? You say you're too old, fat, busy and tired to care about the infinite potential that lurks right where you are sitting now. Do your father's warnings about the risks of starting your own business still ring in your ears? And what about those mortgage payments and the omnipresent seduction of the television set? Throw procrastination a bone and get on with it. "I can't" and "I'm not good enough" are the mantras of the terminally unbloomed. You don't have to quit your job (at least not until you can afford to), but you must be courageous enough to risk a few preliminary falls from perfection.

Whatever you do, wipe your mind clean of any ideas which correlate the pursuit of the dream with shame or failure. You've probably been told, at least once in your life, that if you can't do it right (the first time!), you might as well give it up—*that* dream's just not your cup of tea. Imagine giving away your roller-skates after the first four crashes, or quitting college when it comes time to study James Joyce, or neglecting to ask for that deserved raise because the boss *might* say no.

Fear of failure is the only real failure. Fear teaches you to accept limitations before you've ventured far enough to realize where your true limitations stand. Fear chokes imagination, smashes dreams, and conceals the vital purpose of your life. In learning to fear challenges and short-term failure, you forfeit the prerogative to write, direct and star in the performance entitled *YOUR LIFE.* The proverbial ghost is given up before it's had the pleasure to boogie. But it's not too late: The spirit of life waits just beyond the corner of your doubt.

Globs of perseverance, a pinch of daring, a dash of imagination, and dollops of self-confidence are the ingredients essential to manufacture the dream. The dream requires work, focused will, and steadfast devotion, but the hour a day spent studying for that contractor's license, practicing yoga, penning sonnets, experimenting with watercolors, or preparing gourmet dishes hardly requires sacrificing your children's education or neglecting your spouse. Rather, as your sense of self-fulfillment rises, the general quality of your life will improve. Your work gets smoother, and the kids will learn confidence and creativity by your example.

If luck blows you a kiss, your leisure may become lucrative. That homemaker who's earned neighborhood acclaim for her oatmeal cookies ("love" being the secret ingredient), now sells a hundred bags a week to the local markets, while the accountant, after cutting his workload and living two years on rice and beans, finally finishes a sci-fi novel and receives a big advance. Sure, international recognition may not always ensue, but remember: Happiness resides in the mind of the optimist.

A Late Bloomer myself (Hartmann), it became a habit (an obsession, really) to figure out how old my favorite writers were when they published their first books. In the discovery of a Late Blooming success, I found hope. However, the adventures of relatively unknown Late Bloomers also furnished me with the motivation necessary to persevere in my goals. At restaurants, social functions and seminars, I persuaded bright-eyed people to share their life stories. Bill, a man I met at a public lecture at the Philosophical Research Society, told me a tale worth repeating.

Unaware of any particular aspirations or talents, at twenty-one Bill opted for what seemed a practical route to the so-called good life—the D.D.S. degree. Mom, Dad and Uncle Tom applauded his decision, and years later he passed the state licensing exam, took out a loan and opened a private dental practice.

Just three weeks after his career officially commenced, Bill realized that he hated drilling teeth. At thirty-two, he hadn't a clue about what he wanted to do, but he closed up shop anyway (to the dismay of his family) and began to search his soul. During the three years that followed, he worked as a restaurant manager, a bartender, and a construction worker; he enrolled in a photography class at UCLA extension and photographed his friends for fun. One day his photos won the attention of an acquaintance who subsequently helped him put together a professional portfolio. At forty, Bill makes his living doing what he loves—taking pictures. His dream, not even acknowledged at age thirty, is now reality.

The future rests in the acts of today. In the 1780's Benjamin Franklin wrote that medical science would eventually conquer death along with every other disease. We may still be decades away from over-the-counter immortality drugs; nevertheless, the advent of "longevity" drugs has graduated from the genre of science fiction into the school of science fact, according to some neurochemists. A longer life span may soon be an option for everyone, and longevity will certainly take the pressure off those Late Bloomers who prefer to use time-consuming deductive methods when defining their dreams. Even if longevity drugs aren't your thing, it's wise to keep in mind that more than one M.D. has lectured passionately on the correlation of happiness with a longer, healthier life. (Recent neurophysical research has concluded that mirth helps get the two hemispheres of the brain to work in unison.) And who can deny that a life without dreams is a life lacking joy.

The late Joseph Campbell proclaimed "Follow Your Bliss" as the formula for a vital and successful life. Your bliss is the dream/play/work which provides the song for your soul and the curl for your smile. Without the dream, life loses meaning and purpose. So arise Late Bloomers everywhere! The time is now to follow your dreams, foster your bliss, and join the underground effort to populate the world with smiles. As Tennyson's epic hero Ulysses beckons, "Come, my friends, 'Tis not too late to seek a newer world."

Some Famous Late Bloomers

— Albert Schweitzer had earned an international reputation as an organist and writer of theology by the time he was in his late twenties, but these alone did not suffice to satisfy his soul. At age 30 he entered medical school. Seven years later, with degree in hand, Schweitzer embarked to Africa where he built a hospital. He was awarded the Nobel Peace Prize for his humanitarian work.

— Henry Valentine Miller was thirty-three when he quit his job at Western Union to devote himself to writing, but his acclaimed first novel, *Tropic of Capricorn,* was not published until he was forty-two. Miller also began painting in watercolors at the late blooming age of 37.

— Mohammed, founder of Islam, was first contacted by a messenger of God at age 40 (approximately 610 C.E.); the rest is history.

— Walt Whitman was twenty-nine years old when he put aside a career as a newspaper editor, moved in with his parents, and began writing *Leaves of Grass,* a poem which sings praise of democracy and asserts the beauty of the human body, physical health, and sexuality.

— Mary Baker Eddy, founder of a widespread religious faith known as Christian Science, was fifty-four when she published *Science and Health with Key to the Scriptures,* a book which spelled out the foundations of the system. Eddy suffered from illness throughout her life, found a cure in spiritual healing, and shared her knowledge and experience with the world.

— George Bernard Shaw suffered many literary failures during the early part of his life (his work was said to have "repulsed" all the publishers in London). At age 36, however, he penned his first play which was a small success. Today he is heralded as one of the greatest playwrights of the last 300 years.

— Robert Anton Wilson was over forty when he decided to quit a cushy editorial job and endure poverty so he might write what was to become the cult sci-fi classic *Illuminatus!* and fulfill his dream of becoming a full-time writer.

— Thomas Paine, the political propagandist who paved the way for the American Revolution, was thirty-five when he penned his first pamphlet.

— Timothy Leary, father of the psychedelic revolution, first ingested psychedelic substances (in the form of the sacred mushroom of Mexico) at age forty. Prior to that, he was known to be somewhat "square" in the eyes of his colleagues.

— Leo Buscaglia was over forty and seemingly content with his teaching career when a student of his committed suicide by throwing herself down a cliff, forcing him to ask himself, "What good does teaching someone proper grammar do if it doesn't make them happy." From that Dr. Buscaglia went on to write books which help people become happy.

— Born Anna Mary Robertson, Grandma Moses' fame rests as much on the fact that her talent blossomed at such a late age as it does on the paintings she produced. Moses seriously took up the brush at age 78, when her fingers had become too stiff to pursue the needlework she loved.

— Wallace Stevens, who won the Pulitzer Prize for poetry in 1954, was read by few and only recognized as a major poet late in his life. (He was 35 when his first poems were published.) Stevens held a position in an insurance firm and climbed the proverbial ladder to become vice-president, but continued to write poetry. For him, financial security and the cultivation of the dream were not mutually exclusive.

— Joseph Conrad began working on his first novel at the age of 32, which he completed and published at age 38. Revered as one of the greatest British writers of the twentieth century, many aren't aware that Conrad's native tongue was Polish and that he only became immersed in the English language after he was twenty.

— Lewis Carroll was thirty when he told the story *Alice in Wonderland* to a young girl named Alice Liddell. While Carroll's "profession" was that of a math teacher, his dream had a will of its own and subsequently Alice was written down, revised and subsequently published.

— John Muir is responsible for the establishment of the Sequoia and Yosemite Parks in California. In 1867, at age 29, however, Muir was working on some mechanical inventions, ushering in the Industrial Age, when an accident nearly took out an eye. Muir reevaluated his future, abandoned his career in mechanics, and devoted himself to the exploration of nature. It was no easy task for Muir to talk officials into adopting a forest conservation policy (logging was, and still is, big business), but he relentlessly campaigned for governmental protection. In 1890, when he was 52 years old, his efforts paid off, and the U.S. Congress passed the Yosemite National Park Bill.

— P.D. James, a best-selling mystery writer, started her career at age 46.

❦

The list goes on and on. As model late bloomer, Henry Miller, wrote, "I was cursed or blessed with a prolonged adolescence...[arriving] at some seeming maturity when I was past thirty." Miller referred to himself as the "happiest man alive."

THE ENLIGHTENMENT OF SEX

"Every man a Priest, every woman a Priestess, every home a shrine."
— Timothy Leary

Max, a fifty-seven year old Los Angeles-based artist, was raving about the amazing sex he had had while experimenting with the drug Ecstacy. "My girlfriend became Nefertiti, a goddess. All her imperfections disappeared, and I came for what seemed an eternity. It was heaven." Then he solemnly declared, "When you connect the mind with the heart with the genitals, you find yourself with the power to transform both the world and yourself."

His statement amused me. Max was a down-to-earth Brooklyn Jew who would prefer to see the entire metaphysical community exiled to the land of *Meshugga*, yet his formula of mind + heart + genitals concisely defines the primary aim of sex-centric religions such as Tantra (the Far Eastern version) or Sex Magick (the Western version). Proponents of sacred sex ritual claim that when heart, mind and genitals wed, personal evolution occurs—a transformation from the animal/human into the fully human. From the sex ritualist's point of view, Max's lover did not only *appear* to be an incredible goddess, *she was actually transfigured.* Meanwhile, my Brooklyn friend had temporarily elevated himself into the image of God. Happily, I informed Max that the mystical sex he experienced could be repeated and without ingesting dangerous street drugs. Techniques of Sex Magick and Tantra, once a guarded "inner teaching" in many an occult society or esoteric religion, are now available to the public.

Sexual trends come and go. The 1960s, with the discovery of the Pill, heralded Free Love as essential philosophy; the seventies hyped casual sex as the ultimate lifestyle and the vibrator a mandatory sex tool; the eighties, marked by the onset of AIDS, requested a return to monogamy; and the nineties insisted on putting the sacred back into sexuality. Trek down to any big city bookstore and you'll probably find at least one text covering the ins and outs of ritualistic sex techniques.

Manuals such as Dr. Hyatt's *Secrets of Western Tantra* and *Sex Magic, Tantra and Tarot*; Margo Anand's *The Art of Sexual Ecstasy;*

or Douglas and Slinger's *Sexual Secrets: The Alchemy of Ecstasy* are beginning to usurp the place of classics like *The Joy of Sex* in mainstream stores, while New Age bookstores boast hundreds of titles on the subject. Publications focused exclusively on sacred sex—sporting titles like *"Ecstasy"* and *"Tantra"*—are turning profits. And Tantric workshops abound, ranging from experiential courses in which couples discover touch as a loving language of the soul, to complete vacation seminars offered in Santa Cruz, California, and Maui, Hawaii. And if that weren't enough, performance artist Annie Sprinkle, a former prostitute and porn star, insists that sex led her to spirituality, refers to herself as the Shirley MacLaine of Porn, and promotes "sex as a path to enlightenment. "

A Brief Walk Through the History of Western Sexuality

If Nietzsche were alive today, he might view the sexual/spiritual trend as proof of the cycle of eternal recurrence. History and myth suggest that ritualistic sex (i.e., sex magick) was *the* favorite religion of our pagan ancestors. In fact, the word "lust" in Olde German, meant religious joy and "luster." Long before it became popular to believe that suffering and submission paved the roads to the happy hunting grounds in the sky, sex was the primary means of attaining union and communication with the God/dess of your choice or, less anthropomorphically speaking, "the force which through the green fuse drives the flower" as Delay Thomas so beautifully put it.

The earliest sex rituals intended to invoke the fertility Gods and Goddesses and influence them to give of their bounty. Our ancestors believed that the deities were stimulated by watching their ritualistically performed sex acts (i.e., those performed with *conscious intent*). Early sex magickians counted on the voyeuristic tendencies of the Sky Father and Earth Mother. The stronger the orgasms achieved by the priest and priestesses during the ritual, the better the chance that the Gods and Goddesses would "hear" and be turned on enough to make love, spew seeds, and bless the soil with lush fecundity.

In matriarchical eras, when God was definitively female, it was thought necessary for a man to go through a woman (literally) in order to achieve contact with Deity. Cultures brought up sacred prostitutes as keepers of the Goddesses' temples. Highly respected by their society, these holy whores devoted their lives and bodies to the Goddess and were viewed as "vessels" of the female divinity. They never sold themselves, but chose to give themselves freely, in honor of the Goddess, to those men and women the Goddess deemed worthy. Herodorus wrote that, by law, Babylonian brides would prostitute themselves at the temple for seven days prior to their marriage in order to appease the Goddess, who disapproved of monogamy. Unfortunately, patriarchal religion has relegated woman from an agent of Goddess to an obstacle between man and his God—a demotion which resulted in a split between the Madonna and the whore and, subsequently, a society of sexually neurotic people.

During the Middle Ages, the rising Papal Power gave the practitioners of sex-centric religions a choice: denounce your beloved deities and sexual celebrations, swear to repent your "sins" of the flesh for the rest of your lives, and spend all your waking moments in service under the Will of the One Celibate White Male God or...we'll burn you. But threats can't keep a good thing down, and ritualistic sex moved underground and went occult (which simply means "hidden"). Many medieval "Christian" sects such as the Knights Templar, the "Brothers of the Free Spirit", the Beguines/Beghards, and the Ortlibians were accused and persecuted for practicing sexual ritual.

Most historians propose that Western sex magick was heavily influenced by the Eastern Tantric teachings brought into Europe during the Crusades. During the Renaissance, secret societies, Kabbalah scholarship, and magickal and alchemical arts proliferated, and many of these cults endorsed sex magick as an important, if not basic, factor of their teachings. Alchemy, which most rational-minded folk viewed as the quest of insane men wasting their lives attempting to change lead into gold or concoct immortality elixirs, was particularly ubiquitous.

However, modern researchers—including Carl Jung, Marie Louise Franz and Robert Anton Wilson—theorize that the prized alchemical gold was not a metal at all, but a metaphor for the psyche of the alchemist. And spiritual alchemy can be seen as analogous with sexual alchemy.

For those who knew how to decipher the code, alchemical treatises offered sex-ritual techniques which would, with practice, lead the alchemical mates to "transubstantiation"—or an altered and more integrated state of consciousness. (Like meditation, sex ritual produces a balanced communication between the right and left hemispheres of the brain.) Metaphors pointing toward sexual alchemy are evident in the poems of John Donne—particularly "Love's Alchemy" and "The Ecstasy"—while a careful reading of certain works of Shakespeare, Sir Walter Raleigh, and Sir Phillip Sydney will reveal their awareness of this tradition. The inner teaching of the popular sect of Rosicrucianism are also thought to include sex ritual practices. (The Rosy Cross is itself a sex magick symbol, with its female flower superimposed upon the phallic cross.)

Times have changed and the dogmas invented 2000 years ago have seeped into every crevice of modern social mores. Most of us who were brought up within the net of the Judeo-Christian-Islamic belief system were taught, and accept uncritically, that sex and religion are anathema to each other or, at least, as different as bunnies and rocks.

Judaism placed a taboo on the "wasting" of the holy seed, primarily for the political purpose of propagating the race and manufacturing enough soldiers to ensure its survival. (Some nations today still pay money to women for having children.) Popular Christianity caught the ball of sex, denouncing it as an enemy of religion, and shooting it full of shame and fear. As the philosopher tells us, "Christianity gave Eros poison to drink; he did not die of it but degenerated into a vice." (However, to ward off generalization, it should be noted that Sex magical principles developed within esoteric sects of Christianity, Judaism and Islam.)

Humanity continues to suffer from scores of sexual neuroses. Even now, young girls are forced to repress their sexual urges lest they earn the reputation of "school slut," while teenage boys masturbate to *Playboy* centerfolds in dark closets while sprouting pimples from guilt and anxiety. Consider that such socially harmless pleasures as fellatio, cunnilingus, anal sex, and even sex with a menstruating woman are ostracized to the realms of sin, taboo and, yes, crime. Why should state or church take pains to legislate the styles of love we enact behind closed doors? The sex magician answers quite simply: "In sex is power, a power stronger than the institution and, thereby, dangerous to it."

But Everyone I Know Does It! So Why All The Hoopla?

Even the Bible tells us that sex "is the great mystery." Mysterious or not, our cats and dogs do it without thinking. So just what is going on when two human beings fornicate? Some kind of teleological process unbeknownst to us? The serious play of some celestial genetic engineers? A random game of dice thrown by an insane God/dess or No-One? Perhaps we cannot, at this point in space-time, fathom the mystery, but we can, or so sex magickians tell us, become *involved with mystery.*

The "trick" of successful sex magick lies in the practitioner's ability to maintain consciousness (the faculty which differentiates humans from animals) and "play the energies." In other words, the sex magickian recognizes primal sexual power and employs himself as director of these energies.

Sex magick is distinguished from regular sex primarily in its movement away from the instinctual urge. The ritual intent integrates conscious will with unconscious drive, thereby transforming the instinctual sex drive into something uniquely human. Sex magick teaches complete surrender to the act, the capability to yield to an energy most of us aren't even aware exists within our reach.

It also utilizes techniques which force the mind to stay with the body. In normal sex, most of us drift into fantasy, forfeiting complete bodily awareness and sensation. Sex ritual prohibits sexual fantasy: the mind must remain entirely connected and aware of what's going on both with his own body and that of his partner. Staying entirely present requires discipline and practice, but the results are well worth the effort. The orgasmic blast in a properly done sex ritual is not the "sneeze in the loins" of normal sex, but a total psycho-spiritual-bodily orgasm where everything goes and everything comes. Mystically speaking, this meta-sex orgasm puts the practitioner at one with the Universe.

Is Sex Magick the Ultimate Frontier?

The answer is "yes"—if you believe the ultimate frontier is to be found in accessing the hidden powers of your own mind. Psychologically, Sex Magick and Tantra help cultivate self-mastery. They teach you to clear and focus your mind at will, to prolong concentration, and to meditate. You learn to mentally control your physical body, but also to let go of mind and body completely and surrender fully to ecstasy.

Sex magick practices can be used as a form of psychosexual healing. Focusing on the breath while intoning various sounds or sacred words teaches the couple to consciously manipulate the sexual energy, and eventually, to master it. Creative visualization is practiced and perfected until the movement and flow of energy from one partner to the other is sensed fully. Not surprisingly, couples who practice sex magick or Tantra find themselves in a state of intimacy which they had previously thought impossible.

Traditionally, Western sex magick has been looked upon as evolutionary science—or in modern terminology, a method of accessing neural circuits which have previously lain dormant. As some neuro-physicists have pointed out, we use only a fraction of our brains throughout our lives. Today's adherents of sex magick suggest that their practices promote individual evolution and actual brain change (increasing Theta/Delta waves while decreasing Alpha waves). Indeed, sex ritual seems a more pleasurable way to enlightenment than fasting in a cave in Tibet, and certainly less dangerous than ingesting designer drugs. (Using drugs, particularly psychedelic drugs, as a means to achieve mystic states, generally does not effect permanent transformation, and more often than not, leaves the user in a more depressed state.)

Practicing sex magickians regard themselves as handmaidens of human evolution. Not only do they seek to evolve themselves, many think of themselves as psychopomps, as they claim to participate in the bringing in of souls by concentrating and invoking certain archetypes (usually employing Tarot or Astrological symbolism) with the aim of attracting a specific energy or "soul" to be incarnated as a magical child[1]. In other words, metaphysical eugenics.

In the 1920s, a mystic named Thomas Lake Harris founded a popular cult based on such occult eugenics in Santa Rosa, California, where he intended to test his techniques of "divine respiration" and ecstatic sex ritual. The late Israel Regardie, a neo-Reichian psychotherapist and Kabbalah scholar who strongly influenced contemporary American occultism with his prolific writings and was himself a high-ranking member of the Ordo Templi Orientis (a Tantric sect of which the notorious Aleister

---

[1] The "magickal child" need not be a human child. The term represents any creation or artwork born of the union of the magickian and the archetypal force (or angel) invoked during the sex ritual. For example, a magickian who desires to write a novel might invoke the archetype of Mercury (the Roman god of communication) during the sex ritual and aim to integrate and utilize that force to aid in the fulfillment of his will. The idea of using sex magick to attract a specific energy or "soul" for incarnation has been the goal of many magickal orders.

Crowley was Outer Head), went so far as to suggest that "When better babies are born, Occultism will produce them."

(By the way, occult eugenics has nothing to do with any kind of racial "purification," but rather intends to expedite the natural evolutionary process of humankind.)

While this all may sound a little far-fetched, remember that it's not uncommon for couples to visualize or concentrate on the sex of the desired child when attempting to conceive (and most of us have yelled out "O God" at least once during sexual climax). And some psychologists have even put forth hypotheses which suggest that the moods of the parents during conception affects the fetus. Sex magickians just invoke and visualize on, and with, purpose.

Hardcore sex occultists work to apply this focused energy or power to aid in the fulfillment of their desires. Occult practices such as magick, witchcraft and shamanism presume a sympathetic model of the universe, where basic energies can be manipulated.

When studying the rituals and practices of mystics and shamans throughout the world, Harvard psychologist William James acknowledged that altered states of consciousness are the key to magical powers. Properly done sex ritual produces just such a state. The professional sex magician arouses himself to the point of orgasm, suppresses his climax, and repeats the cycle, and so enters the psycho-spiritual-state which Aleister Crowley termed "eroto-comotose-lucidity." In doing so he believes he has tuned into the Universal Force where, to quote James again, "Actualities seem to float in a wider sea of possibilities from out of which they were chosen." The sex magickian imprints his desire or goal on this wide sea, believing that he has inscribed his will on a "hyperspace" where futures rest ripe for manipulation. Sex magickians don't presume to achieve anything with ritual alone, but claim that ritual combined with actual work proves effective beyond what the work done in the "real" world could effect. Lucky coincidences become a matter of fact.

Sex magick also utilizes erotic energy as a metaphorical sword to slice through the veil of the ego so that the practitioner may attain liberation from the self; however, the release from the bondage of "ego" is usually emphasized as *the goal* in Eastern-styled Tantra, while Western sex magick emphasizes the release from ego as an *opportunity for change* (both of self and circumstance).

Renaissance bards commonly referred to sexual orgasm as "the little death." As many of these poets and playwrights harbored genius, let us suppose, for a moment, that they weren't altogether pulling our legs when they made the analogy between orgasm and death. Perhaps an actual psychic death can occur with total orgasm, and that we can, as novelist D.H. Lawrence suggested when writing of his own sexual experience, immerse ourselves in the "pure, fierce passion of sensuality" so that we may be "burned into essentiality."

As mentioned above, in the prolonged practice of sex magick, lovers accumulate, concentrate and consciously disseminate the sexual energy throughout their entire body. The magickal orgasm is not a release of tension or a physical reflex, but a psycho-spiritual-bodily *blast*—a force potent enough to blow your sense of self away. A psychic rebirth through psycho-sexual healing is possible when in this altered state. This is an excellent time to reprogram yourself in a manner more to your liking as the total orgasm puts you in a state of what psychologists call "imprint vulnerability." While temporarily surrendering the learned self, the unconscious mind is accessed and may be reprogrammed.

So, if you want to replace your habit of ejaculating on your girlfriend's shoes (a desire imprinted during that first masturbation ceremony conducted in the hall closet when you were eleven), with something that won't piss your girlfriend off, try a sex magick ritual. While having sex with your partner, or while masturbating, have an image of the replacement object or act on hand, arouse yourself to eroto-comotose-lucidity and, precisely at the point of orgasm, focus on the object, let it in your mind, let yourself surrender completely to it. Sex magick can enable you to become the metaprogrammer of your own brain, so if you don't succeed the first time, try again. After all, this isn't work, it's sex.

Tantra and Sex Magick are by no means mutually exclusive. To become empowered individually and strengthen the power of will, one must first crack the shell of the conditioned self or cultural programming. Through repeatedly "killing" the ego by way of the total orgasmic blast, the sex magickian finds himself prone to synchronicity, wherein, more often or not, desires seem to be "automatically" fulfilled. Your friends will consider you just plain lucky. It's understandable to be suspicious of something seemingly so archaic and superstitious, but the modern day proponents of sex magick and Tantra are typically professionals with advanced degrees, families, and, yes, successful relationships and amazing sex lives. And, of course, it's always wise to heed the advice of a beautiful alien.

Kim Basinger Knows!

On New Year's Day, 1992, I nursed my hangover by practicing the art of being a couch potato, taking in the popular film *My Stepmother Is An Alien*. In this movie, Kim Basinger plays the part of an extra-terrestrial who is out to get a scientific secret from physicist Dan Ackroyd which would stop the destruction of her planet. In the course of the plot, Ms. Basinger resorts to using sex as a means to get the necessary info from Ackroyd. She's never experienced sex before, but had learned all the right moves during a quick study of one of Ackroyd's porno tapes. What amused and amazed me was Ms. Basinger's remarkable insight concerning the power of sex. Astounded by the energy created during the sexual act, she blurts out, "Think of all the energy produced. Properly channeled that energy could propel half your people out of the galaxy."

Basinger, or more accurately, the author of her dialogue, clues us into the key to successful sex magick—the energy released during sex must be intelligently and willfully channeled. Unaware that such energy exists, much less that we create it, the energy runs amok like Frankenstein's monster, and we become its pawns, serving *it* rather than letting it serve us. (Consider the common phrase, "He's always thinking with his little head.") So perhaps Ms. Basinger only slightly exaggerated when she said that properly channeled sexual energy could propel us out of the galaxy. I have been told by more than one sex magickian that in the ecstasy of orgasm are potential wings which will enable us to fly into yet unexplored space—whether that space be the external universe or the vast beatific mystery of our own minds.

Simple Exercises To Get You Started

Leaving hardcore occultism aside, you can start right now with simple techniques which will invite spirituality into your love-making. Start with deep breathing, filling the stomach first, then the chest. Conscious breathing will help you control and manipulate sexual energies. Annie Sprinkle, Tantric Porn Goddess extraordinaire, claims that it is possible to have an orgasm from breathing alone. "Rhythmic breathing is the best thing since the invention of the vibrator."

After you get the breathing down (more awareness of your *total* body is the first clue), try a preliminary Tantric session with your lover. Begin simply. Remember that orgasm is not the goal here and "all haste is of the devil." It is essential that you take care with the set and setting of the ritual. Clear the room of all clutter, intellectual materials (books and magazines), "things to do" lists, pictures, etc. Light candles and incense, bring in some flowers or a bowl of fruit. Silence is recommended. Bathe separately and don a soft Kimono or robe. White is preferred. It is OK to have one glass of wine, but more than that will inhibit concentration.

Sit directly across from your lover, and let your robes fall from your bodies. Begin breathing, nothing more, with eyes closed. Open your eyes and simply gaze into your lover's eyes. (Gazing is an ancient Tantric practice.) Your breath may synchronize with that of your partner, but don't rush it. This unified breathing ritual will assist you and your partner in releasing extraneous thoughts, old resentments, and distractions which keep you from being fully present. This practice also generates empathy and compassion. Practiced frequently, your relationship will greatly deepen; you may find more understanding and less need for explanation in your daily life.

At first it's best to close the gazing with an embrace and forego normal sexual activity until the next day. (Sex Magick/Tantra is *ritual* sex and entails preparation; it is not meant to be a replacement for normal sex.) After several gazing sessions, add massage to the ritual, beginning with the non-erogenous zones and ending with the more sensitive parts of the body. View your partner as a goddess deserving of your entire attention. She'll catch on and treat every part of your body with the respect, care and attention worthy of a god. You'll probably notice curves, marks, and pleasures of her body which you weren't aware of, even after years of marriage. Again, refrain from normal sexual activity until the next day. Further down the line you will want to incorporate intercourse into your sex ritual. Since there are many different techniques and one thousand and one positions to try out—some boasting cures of everything from a headache to hemorrhoids—the author recommends zooming into the Sex Magick/Tantra section of your favorite metaphysical or occult bookstore, leafing through several books, and choosing whichever book feels sexiest to you. Many of these techniques are clarified in Dr. Hyatt's books, audios and videos.

Eris: Chaos as Prerequisite to Change

"In a dark time, the eye begins to see."
—Theodore Roethke

The goddess Eris is the midwife of Chaos, the bringer of creative destruction. She was heralded in the revolutionary 1960s in the cult book *Principia Discordia.* In this day of increasing social instability, perhaps it would be wise for us to engage her before she drops upon us and surprises us. You might find her a helpful handmaiden, a necessary "evil", and an Archon of CHANGE whose presence is necessary if the world is to break free of what seems, to most spiritually minded people, a pathological society. Let me introduce you to her.

She is not revered for her manners, nor her beauty or grace, and as far as I know, there are no temples or statues or odes in her honor (although she is notably present as the tornado which blew Dorothy out of Kansas). Eris is a messenger of the Crone, in that she serves the crone's destructive wisdom, yet she is not as dark or old or wise as Hecate, but frenzied, flirtatious, quick to anger, mischievous, and "devil may care." Eris is a trickster, a willful reprobate who gets her kicks by shaking things up and stirring the soup. She is the catalytic force of Mary Poppins, who confused the emotionally dead Mr. Banks to the breaking point. Banks then threw off the myopic fetters of the bureaucracy he had enslaved himself with and opened to the love of his family for the first time. Eris was the driving force of Timothy Leary, popularizer of L.S.D., the psychoactive substance which prompted millions to re-examine the belief systems which were handed down pat by the previous generation.

Eris is an anthromorphization of the Tower Card in the Tarot as well as I-Ching hexagram #23: Splitting Apart. Yet, while the Book of Changes tells us that "Splitting Apart means Decay," no one can deny that decaying matter is the source of fertile compost. Likewise, Eris simultaneously brings the sorrows of "letting go" with the joys of creative opportunity. She's about High Risk—a force which aids in the triumph over our limits, boundaries and restrictions.

The Upholders of the Status Quo condemn Eris as a trouble-maker, for she is a goddess of active rebellion. As the driving force of heresy—spiritual, political and social—she takes pleasure in disrupting cultural patterns that have outlived their ability to provide real experience and enthusiastically rejecting the formu-listic or robotic life which stale cultures often produce.

Eris assists evolution, and as she draws her lifeforce from the eternal progression of contraries—worrying not about moral goods and evils—she works day and night to cure stasis of its stiffness. And, while the hardheaded conservative might wage war against the idea that change is the only constant, the modern brain-change technician works to plug into the *Prima Potentia* of Chaos, playing and flirting with Hir maid-of-honor Eris, taking sweet-sour pleasure in the perpetual creation and destruction of perceived reality, death and rebirth.

Eris comes disguised as crisis, but in crisis is opportunity. It is no coincidence that the Chinese symbols for crisis are identical to those for opportunity. The symbols are translated literally as "crisis is an opportunity riding the dangerous wind." Let us then Hail Eris! or, as Marshall McLuhan put it, "BLESS culture shock as dislocation of Mind." Yes, Eris induces culture shock, dislocating the mind and forcing us to discover new meaning, and the symptoms of Breakdown are the harbingers of Breakthrough.

The force of the universe is free and amoral, and like any energy, may be harnessed for evolution or regression, depending on the will of She who knows how to find and use it. It is easy to see why the Status Quo Police (as worshippers of the One and Only Reality) fear and hate the friends of Eris, and are on the march to anathematize the magickians, witches, shamans, *avant garde* artists, film-makers, scientists and computer programmers—those who play in multiple realities—as sinners, criminals, reprobates and children of the devil. Dion Fortune defines evil as "that which is moving in the opposite direction to evolution (and) as the principle of inertia which binds the 'good' the principle of creative movement." In a teleological universe, a universe which is going somewhere, the only evil is stagnancy.

Disobedience is the Greatest Taboo

Eris is famous for indirectly causing the Trojan War. Myth has it that having been intentionally overlooked when the invitations were sent for the wedding of Peleus and Thetis (discord is not a favorite during wedding vows), she disobeyed and crashed the party anyway. Spitefully, she rolled the Apple of Discord across the dance floor. The Apple, as the legend goes, was marked "For the Fairest" and was claimed by Athena, Aphrodite and Hera. Since only one of the three could be *the* fairest, Paris was called to judge the first beauty contest. Aphrodite won by bribing him with the most beautiful woman in the world, Helen of Troy, who was the possession (as women were in those days) of another man. So the Trojan War began.

That Eris' apple-rolling, rather than the lust and desire of Paris, is blamed for the War, seems a tad unfair—a plot more likely to tarnish the name of the midwife of Chaos.

Perhaps it is fitting to make an analogy with a story of another Chaotic midwife, Eve. In the Judeo-Christian tradition it was Eve who abruptly destroyed the Status Quo, the reality, of Eden. Like Eris, Eve rebelled against the gods (yes, gods: the Hebrew word Elohim is plural) by her willful and fateful act of disobedience. Her eating of the infamous apple indirectly caused the exile of herself and her boyfriend Adam from the Garden. The direct cause of exile was the wrath of the gods who didn't want competition from the likes of their creation. So here we are, out of the safe, cultivated, harmonious and static, and into the wild, changing, dangerous and discordant. However, the Wild World Beyond the Garden is THE place where the party is happening, nonstop. Like Joe Campbell said in his conversation with Bill Moyers, "When Eve said yes to the serpent, she said yes to the adventure of life."

Eat an Apple, Open a World

It is interesting to note that Apples play an important role in the stories of both Eris and Eve. Is it only coincidental that an apple, when cut horizontally, reveals the five-pointed star or pentacle (try it yourself)—a symbol feared by the patriarchal systems then and now? (Coincidentally, this chapter is being written on a Macintosh, an Apple computer, which has been programmed to say "Hail Eris!" as an alert signal.)

Many theorists see the myth of The Fall as representative of WoMan's evolutionary move from innocence (blind faith, obedience and dependence) toward experience (consciousness, the ability to self-reflect, and the will to change and create change); thus interpreted, "falling" was a very fortunate move, a rite of passage, an opportunity to come into our own. Similarly, Humpty's "great" fall, can be read "great" meaning "terrible" or "great" meaning "supreme", "fortuitous", or "wonderful". And even though War is never pleasant, the battle of Troy was the catalyst for much change and progress (not to mention a fertile sea of archetype and myth from which artists and poets of past and present might fish). As pulleys of the rope of time and change, reality makers and brain-change technicians can't afford to waste time quibbling about what is "right" and what is "wrong." To eat beef in India is sin; to eat beef in Texas makes you a real man! If we are not moving forward, we are moving back.

Eris is a Friend to the Brain-Change Technician

Occult magick, witchcraft and shamanism are concerned with the re-ordering of reality through the re-ordering of consciousness and the accessing of will. The magickian aims to change self, consciousness, and/or peripheral reality in accord with will. Through magickal practice and ritual, the magickian aims to cultivate the consciousness necessary to manifest such change.

Most occult practices presume a sympathetic model of the universe—a web of life, if you like. The idea that basic energies can be manipulated is based on the realization that from a certain dimension, or when in a more "sensitive" state of perception, all things are interconnected—the paradoxical idea that we are One yet Many. While in the reality-tunnel of our "normal" state of consciousness, we believe ourselves as autonomic, individual and un-connected to the whole. But it is not far-fetched to entertain the concept that we are as yet unable to perceive "higher" levels of existence.

Consider a model world called Flatland. Flatland is two-dimensional and populated by squares who know left and right, and back and forth (i.e., width and length), but cannot fathom the three-dimensional attribute of up and down (height). Edwin Abbott, a Shakespearian scholar, tells an amusing fiction set in Flatland which illustrates some possible problems we might face when questioning so-called extra-dimensional or divine communication. Paraphrased, the story goes:

One lovely day a three-dimensional creature is flying above Flatland and sees a congenial looking square entering a house. The 3-D creature decides to say hello, but the Flatlander cannot see the creature who is hovering above his house and hears the voice seemingly coming from within himself. He questions his sanity. The 3-D creature is irritated at being called a figment of imagination and decides to fly beneath the square and kick the Flatlander into this alternative dimension called UP. The Flatlander floats in UP for an ecstatic while before dropping back into his own 2-Dimensional world. He tries to explain to his friends that he had ventured into some "mystic" dimension called UP. Of course, the fellow Flatlanders, having no such experience, pat the poor deranged fellow on the back and suggest a visit to the local psychiatrist.

You get the picture.

Vacationing in Alternity

When you alter your reality through ritual, sex, drugs, sensory deprivation, or what you will, "normal" reality ceases to be and we can access a seemingly "mystic" dimension, whether it be a dimension of the mind or an actual dimension of space—an "alternity" to use the term coined by Dr. John Lilly to describe such states. Magicians and Shamans of yore knew that too much time spent in the mundane world and "normal" consciousness would cause them to "forget" alternity and thus sabotage the success of their magick, whether it be healing, precognition or controlling weather. They knew that the common worldview of individual separateness worked as a wall to block the underlying magickal sympathetic reality while bombarding them with doubt, interference, reactionary thinking and criticism. That is why they took care to break routine now and then by incorporating into their lifestyles such acts as fasting in the desert, strange rites, ingestion of drugs, vision quests, prolonged sexual abstinence and/or activity, and even masochism. Harvard psychologist William James believed altered states of consciousness to be the key to magical powers, the key to becoming the artist of our own lives. Altered states lets us put off the cloak of culture and tune into the primary self where the future rests ripe for manipulation, if you will. Dr. James said, "Actualities seem to float in a wider sea of possibilities from out of which they were chosen." Who has done the choosing: you, your mom, your government, your teacher? Who will do the choosing in the future?

Magickal reality presupposes the existence of a free-for-all power source—that "divine" energy which has its center everywhere and circumference nowhere—variously called the Archetypal World, the lifeforce, Void, Atman, Tao, Anima Mundi, Spirit, Chaos, God, etc. This is the stuff from which magic, inspiration and genius stem. It is the thread which connects us to the ancient mind, the Great Memory, the Akashic Records, or the Aboriginal Dreamtime, holding the potential of future as well as the tapestry of the past. It is the force which, upon amalgamation and application of conscious will, allows us to speak the language of our primal ancestors: animals, insects, plants, algae, stones, rivers and, earlier still, the stars, and, perhaps even to communicate with our future selves.

Shakespeare, the enigmatic playwright (or corporation of playwrights as the controversy goes), is (are) said to be linked to the secret societies which flourished during the Renaissance period. Many agree that Shakespeare hid occult knowledge within his (their) plays, and while studying him in graduate school, I attended to culling any occult material I could. I found a lot, but most relevant to this article is the comedy "As You Like It" which, to me, confirms the "magickal" idea that communication with Gaia, or the Big Mind of Universe, is achieved by shucking off the mask of culture. In the play, Touchstone, the Archetypal Wise Fool, tells us that when he is "exempt from the public haunt he might find tongues in trees, books in running brooks, sermons in stones and good in everything."

The Science of Reprogramming Your Self

We hold the information of the Universe within our DNA. It makes sense that we should be capable of accessing this information by turning on the as yet untapped circuits of our neural system. That humans have evolved to a point where they must take responsibility for further evolution of the species—intentional evolution—is a controversial, but fascinating, concept which has interested scientists, intellectuals and mystics as varied as Gurdjieff, Aldous Huxley, George Bernard Shaw, Jean Houston, John Lilly and Aleister Crowley.

The film *Altered States* depicts the protagonist, a scientist very loosely modeled on Dr. John Lilly, travelling backwards through his genetic memory as he experiments with sensory deprivation tanks combined with neuro-active chemicals. He devolves into apeman, and further into an amorphous blob of pulsating energy—pure chaos.

Real-life experiments conducted by Dr. Lilly suggested that it is possible to "visit" our selves in various states of evolution, but of course physical transformation did not occur. It was the mind which took a ride on a genetic elevator of sorts, allowing recognition and realization of the primeval and/or cosmic consciousness. The point is that we can access the Self beneath the programming and choose to change our minds/realities. We can become the meta-programmers of our brains rather than the puppets of the culture by applying the magickal formula: Will + Imagination + Altered States.

The inter-connected model of the universe—or web of life—is no longer limited to those of a mystical/magickal mindset, but is also a model chosen by many internationally recognized physicists as it works in accord with the Quantum Inseparability Principle. Bell's Theorem puts forth the concept of non-locality, which notes that on a sub-atomic level every particle is connected to every other particle. The idea of information being able to "travel" faster than light or "information without transportation" seems to support the concepts of synchronicity, magickal coincidence, and telepathy. Dr. David Bohm speculates that the universe might not only prove to be non-local, but holographic as well. This model fits perfectly with the age-old idea that WoMan, along with everything else in the world, is a microcosm of the whole, containing all the information of the whole—past, present and future.

"As above, so below" says the Emerald Tablet of Hermes Trimegestis, while Carl Sagan tells us that "the very matter that makes us up was generated long ago in red giant stars." We, along with the blade of grass and the fierce tiger, are literally the children of stars. As within, so without. One need only plug into Source to know it, to play it, to create with it, to become alike to the very god/desses we have for so long projected onto the images we worship.

Summon Eris, Experience Life

Mystics, magickans and brain-change technicians alike employ ritual to invoke the archetypal mind (which is simply the art of tuning into those "cosmic" signals we normally edit), and to expose and make accessible our power source—the potential energy of Chaos. We enter a "non-local" state where our definitions of reality, our masks of personality, temporarily fall away. Who we believe we are at any given moment is always fiction, for we are another thing a moment later; or as W.B. Yeats implied, we cannot "know the dancer from the dance."

Eris aids in dissolving the protective circle of self-concept by scrambling our programs, confusing us, and ferrying us into the space of No-Form, the lap of Chaos. Hence, we find ourselves in reach of magickal power, in a state of trance, ready to dance a new reality for ourselves. As William Burroughs astutely commented, "Escape routes open in times of chaos."

Emptied of prior definition and highly impressionable, we use whatever means or rituals we choose to change the station to a reality more in accord with our will, or create a wholly new one. Brain-change technicians are meta-programmers who dance through dozens of virtual realities. We re-program ourselves, clothing ourselves with new belief systems or realities as creatively and as often AS WE WILL. (As I see it, the more often we change, the faster we evolve.)

As we crucify the false self and move through the processes of dis-identification and re-definition of our perceived realities, our normal reality changes to a magical reality. We become PRESENT. We soon recognize that we are free to be the dancer when we dance, the worker when we work, and the player when we play.

Formal ritual performed in this Concept-Free state, whether Crowley-style invocations or a Catholic Exorcism, has a high success rate, evoking or invoking what spirits, angels, demons, gods, or goddesses, in the form and style you expect, and as you will. Plugged into the source of your power—the Chaotic Pool of Potentia—you may employ the force of concentrated will, imagination, and archetypal symbols to "charge" your magical tools, talismans and amulets. Then, simply project your desire into the Cornucopian Womb of the Universe. Remember, your "tools" could be pen, hammer or guitar. One of my magical tools is my computer.

Your authentic will is very effective when applied in the dimension of potential (i.e., Chaos), more so, I think, than when applied to the denser astral or physical planes where it can be refracted by opposing wills or sabotaged by your own reactionary mental processes. Your magic will work, so be certain that you want that which you will. Also, it helps to have some sort of symbol of your desire at hand to concentrate upon or verbalize—a word or mental image will do—so you won't need to regain "normal" consciousness in order to remember the purpose of your ritual. Formal invocations should be memorized.

How Shall I Invoke Thee?
Many and Mischievous are the Ways

There are thousands of ways to invoke Eris. You might devote yourself to meditation on the TOWER card, or better yet, draw or paint your own. It helps to get out of your head where all of your programs, as well as the potential re-actions to your current programs and future programs, exist. Forget the mind; get into your body instead. Prior to practicing brain-change rituals, prepare yourself and your space by breaking apart "normal" reality.

Perform a frenzied Erisian dance, whirling like a crazy dervish until you don't know which way is which, stand on your head for an hour, indulge in extended sexual practice or Tantra (prolonged sexual activity is perhaps the simplest and most pleasurable way to alter consciousness), or have sex with an unusual person under unusual circumstances. Throw yourself into an extreme emotional state (terror, devotion or anger), drum until you become the beat, give your ear to dissonant music, or stare at a cubist painting until you understand it. Hold your breath or try Kriya Yoga techniques. Laugh for the sake of laughter and nothing else (try listening to the song "I Love to Laugh" on the *Mary Poppins* soundtrack for a couple hours). Talk gibberish or practice Socratic dialectic with yourself.

Invoking Eris in your daily life will take some of the tedium out of mundane tasks and greatly speed up your passage into a magical multiple reality. A good way to start is to break habits and replace them with new ones, then break the new habits and replace them, and so on. Or walk in a different way, talk to strangers, act "out of character" (tell your friends you're "performing an experiment"), wear clothing which is not your style, explore new routes to work, eat exotic foods, eat on the floor, eat without utensils, write with the hand you don't write with, try to believe in ideas you abhor (except during elections), make love to someone who is not your "type".

Making love with "unattractive" partners has been a favored method of self-concept disintegration for at least one notorious brain-change expert. Kissing a leper was a mystical experience for one beloved Saint. When pleasure is combined with repulsion, two contrary values are married, your judgment is dissolved, and you are lifted beyond duality into oneness.

As you give your former "static" reality various Erisian jolts, make sure you continuously question your beliefs about the world, your ideas of your self, your goals and desires. Be brutally "honest" with yourself and beg your friends to do the same. Find out where you are and why; *you* can search your "soul" more effectively than any therapist. What is important is that you 1) recognize the foundations, scaffolds and walls of your "normal" reality, and 2) demolish them and build anew. To maintain residence in magical reality, keep changing the channel, again and again and again. If you're not moving forward, you're moving backwards! Evolve!

As we become expert brain-change technicians and enter the realm of magic, synchronicities become common occurrences and wishes begin to come true so frequently that one refrains from wishing carelessly. Things just fall into place. Thus, we no longer have to put aside time specifically for such practices; instead, we live magically. Eris, as the midwife of Chaos, helps to provide us with the necessary dis-orientation and disillusionment, both in our rituals and our everyday lives, so we may more easily cast off the shells which separate our essential spark, in all its marvelous and ancient luminosity, from that of everything else in the universe. And so we realize that "All the World's a Stage" and "Every Man and Every Woman is a Star." We become the directors, producers and artists of our lives.